Middle East Studies
Monograph Series

As part of its mission to broaden U.S. Marine Corps access to information and analysis through publishing, Middle East Studies at Marine Corps University (MES) has established different mechanisms to disseminate relevant publications, including a Monograph Series. The aim of the MES Monograph Series is to publish original research papers on a wide variety of subjects pertaining to the Middle East and South and Central Asia. The focus of the Monograph Series is on timely subjects with strategic relevance to current and future concerns of the U.S. Professional Military Education community.

The seventh issue of the MES Monograph Series features an expanded and revised edition of Monograph Number 1, published in August 2011. Mr. Michael Eisenstadt has updated his arguments and analysis based on the major changes that have taken place in the Islamic Republic of Iran since 2011, specifically the nuclear agreement and Iran's expanded military and political roles the region and beyond. I am thankful to Mr. Eisenstadt for his continued support of the MES mission through his presentations and writings.

We welcome comments from readers on the content of the series as well as recommendations for future monograph topics.

Amin Tarzi
Director, Middle East Studies
Marine Corps University

DISCLAIMER

The Strategic Culture of the Islamic Republic of Iran: Religion, Expediency, and Soft Power in an Era of Disruptive Change

by Michael Eisenstadt

AUTHOR'S PREFACE TO THE EXPANDED AND REVISED SECOND EDITION

This expanded and revised edition of "The Strategic Culture of the Islamic Republic of Iran," first published by Marine Corps University in 2011, sharpens, fleshes out, and updates analyses and arguments presented in the original edition.

In the wake of the nuclear deal between the P5+1/EU and Iran (known formally as the Joint Comprehensive Plan of Action), and in light of the Islamic Republic's growing role in the Middle East, the need for such a publication is greater than ever before. It is my hope that this monograph will fill the need for a primer on the strategic culture of the Islamic Republic of Iran (IRI) that will provide insights into the factors shaping its regional conduct.

Analysts, strategists, and policymakers are told to never "mirror image" when considering the conduct of another country, but they are never told what "image" to put in its place. This publication constitutes an attempt to convey the essential elements of the strategic culture of the IRI to assist these respective communities create an alternative image of "the other."

It also represents an attempt to inject culture into the debate about strategy and policy. After more than a decade of combat in Afghanistan and Iraq, the US military understands very well the importance of factoring culture into tactical and operational planning.[1] But there are few signs of a similar recognition of the importance of cultural understanding among planners and policymakers at the strategic and national levels. This monograph attempts to rectify this shortcoming.

That said, as critical as cultural understanding is, the strategic culture approach is not a single factor explanation for, or the "key" to understanding the IRI's strategic behavior. The factors shaping Iranian foreign and defense policy cannot be reduced to a single variable. Personality, politics, and competing perceptions of the expediency of the regime and/or the national interest all play critical roles—though strategic culture may influence all of these. For that reason, I believe that the strategic culture approach provides particularly useful insights into how the IRI's leadership sees the world, and why they do what they do.

Although this monograph refers to "the" strategic culture of the IRI, the latter is not necessarily a monolith. It is possible that various government officials and entities may hold divergent approaches regarding some of the topics dealt with here, just as there are differences and debates in any country about these matters. But within "the system," there seems to be little disagreement over fundamentals; this publication provides a composite sketch, drawn from numerous sources, of the IRI's fundamental approach to deterrence, defense, and the use of force.

The IRI's strategic culture marked a distinct break with the strategic culture of Iran under Mohammad Reza Shah's rule, which was heavily influenced by Western thought and practice. And while it did not emerge from the revolution fully formed, it has shown a remarkable degree of continuity—a testament to the degree to which it is rooted in and reflects the ideology and values of the revolution. Nonetheless, there are also important elements of continuity in the policies of the Shah's Iran and the Islamic Republic, particularly the drive for regional dominance in accordance with geopolitical, as opposed to ideological considerations.

Yet, the IRI's strategic culture is neither static nor immutable. Since 2011, Iran's circumstances have been transformed: the United States now faces an increasingly confident and assertive Iran, imbued with an unprecedented sense of agency, due in part to its success in expanding its regional influence, and its role in ensuring the survival of its principal regional ally—Bashar al-Asad's Syria. In just a few years, Iran has gone from:

- Fearing strategic encirclement by the United States in the wake of the latter's invasion of Afghanistan (2001) and Iraq (2003), to practicing encirclement of the Gulf states and Israel;

- A strategically lonely power, to the leader of the region's most cohesive bloc, the so-called "axis of resistance." However, Syria, formerly an able partner, is now a dependent rump state, while Russia's continued support for the Asad regime is uncertain;

- An insurgent state that seeks to subvert the Arab state system, to a state that continues to practice subversion, but which has also had to learn how to successfully wage counterinsurgency to assist its Syrian and Iraqi allies against armed opposition groups. These include salafi-jihadist organizations such as the self-described Islamic State (IS);

- A state whose preferred means of projecting influence was through "soft power" (enabled by "hard power") to a state that now pursues a more balanced "soft/hard power" strategy;

- A nuclear rogue state, to a nuclear threshold state whose status as such has been confirmed and legitimized by the leading members of the international community.

As a result of these dramatic changes, elements of Iran's strategic culture may now be in flux, even if its overall approach remains unchanged. Understanding the factors shaping the IRI's strategic conduct will remain critical for the United States and its allies, whether or not the nuclear accord recently concluded with the Islamic Republic is actually implemented, or achieves its intended objectives.

I am delighted that Middle East Studies at Marine Corps University has agreed to publish an expanded and revised edition of this monograph, which I hope will inspire further research on this topic, provide deeper insight into the logic guiding Tehran's strategic behavior, and better prepare analysts, strategists, and policymakers to deal with the challenges posed by the Islamic Republic.

Finally, it is my heartfelt wish—for the sake of all the peoples of the Middle East—that this monograph will soon become outdated because Iran is no longer a state that routinely violates the rights of its citizens, threatens its neighbors, and calls for "Death to America." But until that day comes, it is my hope that this monograph will help planners and policymakers in their efforts to navigate the complex and fraught US-Iran relationship.

Michael Eisenstadt
Washington, DC
October 2015

INTRODUCTION

The Islamic Republic of Iran (IRI) is an unconventional adversary that requires unconventional approaches to planning, strategy, and policy. These approaches must take into account the country's sophisticated culture, the regime's religious-ideological orientation, the abiding importance of Iranian nationalism, and Iran's modern military history. And they must recognize the IRI's unique approach to statecraft, strategy, and the use of force.

Doing so is no easy task for Americans, as the United States and Iran are studies in opposites when it comes to culture, values, and politics: [2]

- The United States is a secular republic whose public life is, nonetheless, suffused with religious language and symbolism, whereas the Islamic Republic is a theocracy whose policies are based on the essentially secular principles of the "expediency of the regime" and the national interest.

- Americans are often willing to compromise on principles to achieve results, whereas Iranians often believe that sticking to one's principles is the way to achieve results.

- Americans value forthrightness, while Iranians are often reticent about revealing motives or intentions to others.

- The United States is a soft-power dynamo that tends to think in hard-power terms, while Iran values soft power above all else and as a result, tends to fixate on alleged American soft-warfare threats.

- While American generals and policymakers think largely about achieving physical effects, their Iranian counterparts are often more concerned about moral and psychological effects.[3]

These factors complicate efforts to understand Tehran's behavior and to formulate effective policies toward the Islamic Republic.

Iran's political system, moreover, is unique in that it is characterized by parallel structures that are the locus of multiple power centers. These consist of both traditional state and revolutionary institutions: the President and Supreme Leader; the Majles and Guardian Council; the Judiciary and Special Clerical Courts; and the regular military and the Islamic Revolution Guard Corps (IRGC), with the former often counterbalanced, and sometimes undermined by the actions of the latter.[4] This organizational complexity and the importance of informal influence networks[5] also often renders the functioning of the regime opaque—even to many of its own members—making it especially difficult for outsiders to understand what is going on.

Finally, planners and policymakers dealing with the IRI should keep in mind three generalizations that can be said of a number of countries, but which are especially true for the Islamic Republic:

- Nothing in Iran is as it seems; things are often to the contrary. Certainty regarding intentions, power relationships, and decision making processes and outputs is often elusive;

- Nothing in Iran is black and white; ambiguity and shades of grey rule. This is both a defining characteristic of Iranian culture, and a reflection of the fact that ambiguity is often used by the regime as a stratagem to confound its enemies;

- Iranian politics are characterized by numerous contradictions and paradoxes. Do not seek consistency where none exists.

With these caveats in mind, this monograph will attempt to identify the salient features of the IRI's strategic culture, and their implications for planning, strategy, and policy.[6]

A NATION OF MARTYRS?

Any attempt to understand the national security policies of the IRI must start by clearing up a range of misconceptions regarding the religious and ideological mainsprings of Iranian behavior, which have prevented clear-headed thinking about Iran over the past three decades.

Because Shi'ite religious doctrine is central to the official ideology of the Islamic Republic and exalts the suffering and martyrdom of the faithful, Iran is sometimes portrayed as an irrational, "undeterrable" state with a high pain threshold, driven by the absolute imperatives of religion, rather than by the pragmatic concerns of statecraft.

This impression has been reinforced by Iran's use of costly human-wave attacks during the Iran-Iraq War, its unnecessary prolongation of the war with Iraq in pursuit of the overthrow of Saddam Hussein (and the "liberation" of Jerusalem thereafter), and its support for groups that pioneered the tactic of the suicide bombing—such as the Lebanese Hizballah and the Palestinian Islamic Jihad.

Iranian officials deliberately cultivate and play up this image of Iran as a dangerous foe whose soldiers seek martyrdom, and whose society is willing and able to pay any price. They do so not only because it reflects the regime's idealized self-image and view of Iranian society, but also to energize the regime's hard-core support base, to intimidate its enemies, and to strengthen the country's deterrent posture.

This is, however, an anachronistic view of Iran. Iranian propaganda, enduring memories of human wave attacks, and Iranian-sponsored suicide bombings have done much to distort thinking about Iran. In the heady, optimistic, early days of the revolution, the Iranian people were indeed willing to endure hardships, make great sacrifices, and incur heavy losses in support of the war effort—with Tehran eschewing the opportunity for a cease-fire in 1982 to pursue the overthrow of the Baathist regime in Baghdad and to export the revolution beyond.

But as the war with Iran dragged on, popular support for it waned. The population became demoralized and wearied by years of inconclusive fighting, making it increasingly difficult to attract volunteers for the front. Many clerics came to the conclusion that the war was unwinnable.[7] As a result, the regime had to abandon its slogan of "war, war until victory," and Ayatollah Ruhollah Khomeini had to agree to "drink from the poisoned chalice" in accepting the cease-fire with Iraq in July 1988. As it turned out, Iran was not—as Ayatollah Khomeini was fond of saying—"a nation of martyrs."

Since then, within the context of a relatively activist foreign policy, Iranian decision-makers have generally shunned direct confrontation, and have tended to act through surrogates (such as the Lebanese Hizballah) or by means of stealth (Iranian small boat and mine operations against shipping in the Gulf during the Iran-Iraq War), in order to manage risk. Such behavior is evidence of an ability to engage in rational calculation, to accurately assess power relationships, and to identify means to circumvent adversary "red lines."[8] Indeed, this is one of the striking paradoxes of the IRI's leadership: while it has demonstrated a pronounced tendency toward paranoia and conspiratorial thinking,[9] it has also frequently shown an ability to engage in fairly subtle calculation.

Though its Lebanese Hizballah client pioneered the suicide bombing in the early 1980s, it has been years since Iran's proxies have employed this tactic. While continuing to cultivate the spirit of resistance, jihad, and martyrdom, Hizballah by and large abandoned suicide bombings in the late 1980s,[10] opting for more conventional military tactics, while Iran's various 'special groups' proxies in Iraq, such as Asaib Ahl al-Haqq and Kataib Hizballah, have eschewed suicide bombing in favor of explosively formed penetrator (EFP), mortar, and rocket attacks.[11] Today, it is Sunni jihadist groups such as al-Qaeda and its affiliates, IS, and until relatively recently, the Jundallah organization in Iran, whose preferred tactic is the suicide bombing.

Tehran's cautious behavior during a number of crises since the end of the Iran-Iraq War is the best proof that Iran has generally sought to avoid direct involvement in costly conflicts and quagmires with its enemies, even at the cost of overlooking the revolution's fundamental ideological tenets. Thus, even though the Iranian constitution enjoins the IRI to support the world's oppressed (*mostaz'afin*) against their oppressors (*mostakbirin*), Iran abandoned beleaguered Shi'ite communities to their fates, rather than enter into potentially risky and costly foreign adventures during the 1991 Shi'ite uprising in Iraq, the 1998 capture of the city of Mazar-e-Sharif by the Afghan Taliban (which led to the slaughter of thousands of Shi'ite Hazaras as well as the murder of eight Iranian diplomats and a journalist), the 2006 war between Israel and the Lebanese Hizballah, and the 2011 crackdown on mainly Shi'ite protestors in Bahrain.[12]

Instead, in each of these cases, Iran responded in a token manner or belatedly, often by indirect means or proxies; it sent members of the Iraqi Badr Corps to participate in the 1991 Shi'ite uprising in Iraq, armed the Afghan Northern Alliance against the Taliban, rebuilt the Lebanese Hizballah after the 2006 war, and attempted to recruit a Mexican narco-terrorist to assassinate the Saudi ambassador in Washington, DC in 2011, to avenge Saudi Arabia's role in quashing unrest in Bahrain.

In each of these cases the Islamic Republic showed that it is not insensitive to risks and costs—although in several, war parties argued for intervention. Such pragmatism is consistent with the principle of the "expediency of the regime" (*maslahat-e nizam*) that was established by the founder of the Islamic Republic, Ayatollah Khomeini, as the precept ultimately guiding domestic and external policy-making in the IRI.[13]

Khomeini set down this principle in a series of letters to then President Ali Khamenei and the Council of Guardians in December 1987 and January 1988, respectively, in which he affirmed the Islamic Republic's authority to destroy a mosque or suspend the observance of the five pillars of faith (the fundamentals of Muslim observance) if the interests of the regime so required.[14] The Expediency Council, established in February 1988, was created to help the Supreme Leader discern the interests of the regime. This axiom has guided Iranian decision-making ever since.

Indeed, Ayatollah Khomeini referenced the concept of *maslahat* in explaining his acceptance of the cease-fire ending the Iran-Iraq War—explaining that it was "based only on the interest of the Islamic Republic."[15] In establishing this principle, Khomeini formalized the supremacy of *raison d'état* over the tenets of Islam as the precept guiding Iranian decision-making. This dictum guides decision making at the highest levels of the regime, as well as the actions of the regime's foot-soldiers.[16]

The assumption underpinning this precept is that the regime's brand of revolutionary Islam will not survive unless the IRI survives.[17] The preservation of the Islamic Republic is thus the ultimate religious value, and it becomes permissible to do all sorts of things, including torture and murder, and to violate the tenets of Islam, in order to preserve the regime. Paradoxically, when it comes to the interests or survival of the regime, policymaking in the theocratic IRI is based on the secular principle of *raison d'état*, rather than the dictates of the regime's ideology or the tenets of Shi'ite Islam.

Thus, despite the frequent resort to religious allusions and imagery in speeches and interviews, Iranian officials often employ the language of deterrence theory as spoken and understood in the West. For instance, shortly after the first test launch of the *Shihab-3* missile in July 1998, then Defense Minister Ali Shamkhani explained that to bolster Iran's deterrent capability

> we have prepared ourselves to absorb the first strike so that it inflicts the least damage on us. We have, however, prepared a second strike which can decisively avenge the first one while preventing a third strike against us.[18]

The IRI, however, views these concepts through a uniquely Iranian lens which is shaped by a conspiratorial worldview and harnessed to an anti-status quo policy agenda, posing unique challenges to deterrence.

Notwithstanding its generally cautious approach in the defense and foreign-policy arenas, the IRI has occasionally taken potentially self-defeating or risky actions, some entailing a heightened possibility of military confrontation, revealing an erratic streak in its behavior.[19] Thus, it:

- Facilitated Hizballah's bombing of the US Embassy in Beirut (April 1983), and the US Marine and French paratrooper barracks in Beirut (October 1983);[20]

- Facilitated Hizballah's bombing of the Israeli embassy and a Jewish community center in Buenos Aires (March 1992 and July 1994, respectively);[21]

- Assassinated Iranian Kurdish oppositionists in a Berlin restaurant, leading to a rift with the European Union (September 1992);[22]

- Commissioned the bombing of the US military barracks (Khobar Towers) in Dhahran, Saudi Arabia by Saudi Hizballah (June 1996);[23]

- Seized fifteen British sailors and Marines conducting maritime security operations in the Shatt al-Arab and held them for over a week (March 2007);[24]

- Plotted to assassinate the Saudi ambassador to the US in Washington, DC (March-September 2011);[25]

- Acquiesced in, and perhaps encouraged the occupation of the British embassy in Tehran by a mob (November 2011), despite the international condemnation of Iran's occupation of the US embassy three decades prior, and;[26]

- Launched a terrorist attack against the Israeli embassy in New Delhi (February 2012), even though India had consistently resisted US efforts to sanction Iran's oil sector.[27]

Because none of these actions prompted a direct military riposte or serious retribution by any of the countries involved, the IRI's leadership may believe that Iran can get away with occasional bouts of reckless behavior that challenge international norms. This explains, in part, why relations with Iran have always been so fraught, complicated, and unpredictable.

DEFENSE PLANNING

The IRI's defense planning is driven by a powerful desire to: 1) enhance its status by transforming Iran into a regional power capable of projecting influence throughout the Middle East and beyond; 2) avoid a repeat of the tragic deterrence failure that led Iraq to invade Iran in 1980—a trauma that affects Iran to this day, and; 3) achieve self-reliance in all areas of national life—a fundamental goal of the Islamic revolution.

To this end, the Islamic Republic seeks to avoid or deter conventional conflict, while advancing its anti-status quo agenda via proxy, and information (i.e., psychological warfare) operations, combining hard and soft power to shape the regional and global environment in ways conducive to its interests.[28]

Status and Influence. The IRI's leadership believes that the Islamic Republic has a key role to play in world affairs as the standard bearer of revolutionary Islam and the guardian of oppressed Muslims (and non-Muslims) everywhere. They are convinced that the fate of the *ummah* (the Islamic community) depends on Iran's ability to transform itself into a major power that can defend and advance the interests of that community. This perception also leads Tehran to support radical Islamic movements throughout the Middle East, to undermine the interests of its principal adversaries in the region—particularly Israel, Saudi Arabia (its main rival for leadership of the Islamic World), and the United States, to reshape the international environment in a way conducive to Iranian interests, and to burnish the regime's revolutionary Islamic credentials at home and abroad. This claim to leadership causes Iran to present itself in non-sectarian terms—

Michael Eisenstadt

not as the leader of the world's Shi'ites, but of the world's Muslims. (In recent years, it has increasingly emphasized its anti-imperialist and anti-Western credentials as well, in order to garner support from Muslim and non-Muslim states and movements that seek to overturn the existing world order.)[29]

This universalistic Islamic impulse has coexisted uneasily with Iranian nationalism, and each has, at different times, exerted varying degrees of influence over Iranian foreign policy. The Islamic tendency generally dominated in the 1980s, while Islamic and nationalist orientations have contended with each other since then. The tension between Islam and nationalism continues to this day, as witnessed by increasingly frequent references by Iranian officials in recent years to the national interest as a principle guiding Iranian foreign policy. This enduring tension, however, is a manifestation of the IRI's inability to decide "whether it is a nation or a cause," as Henry Kissinger so astutely put it.[30]

Iran's leadership has always believed that the IRI is the dominant power in the Gulf by dint of geography, demography, resource endowments, and a specifically Iranian sense of manifest destiny. This translates into a desire to control the Gulf militarily, to deny its use by others if need be, and to defend its vital interests and assert its rights in the Gulf against rivals, such as Saudi Arabia and the United States.

It believes, moreover, that the political and economic order that underpinned US power since World War II is in crisis and that the United States is a power in decline, while Iran is a rising power. Accordingly, it has attempted to establish alliances with other anti-status quo powers (such as Venezuela and Russia) that seek to constrain American power, in order to hasten this decline. It likewise believes that Israel and the Gulf states are doomed to fail.

More recently, senior Iranian officials have depicted Iran as the dominant power in the Middle East, whose influence extends to four Arab capitals (Beirut, Damascus, Baghdad, and Sanaa), and which is well on the way to building a modern-day Iranian empire whose influence will be felt throughout the Middle East.[31] These statements, however, were criticized by some Iranians who may have felt that it was impolitic to say out loud what many Iranians think—or at least would like to believe.

There has long been a significant gap between the self-image and the aspirations of the regime, and the reality of Iran's conventional military weakness. Tehran has attempted to close this gap by taking steps to expand and modernize its conventional forces, though financial constraints, US pressure on potential arms suppliers, and other priorities limited its ability to do so. As a result, the IRI has focused on developing niche capabilities that exploit adversary vulnerabilities and Iran's geographic position (especially its proximity to the Strait of Hormuz)[32] and that provide the biggest "bang for the buck": proxy forces, naval anti-access capabilities, and rockets/missiles. And it has created the infrastructure needed to eventually produce nuclear weapons.

Iran has done relatively well, given its relatively modest investment in conventional forces since the end of the Iran-Iraq War. And its effective use of proxies following the Arab uprisings has enabled it to greatly extend its reach and influence in the region. It has, however, reportedly increased its defense budget by 32.5 percent in the 2015-2016 fiscal year, allocating much of it to the purchase of missiles and conventional arms, perhaps in anticipation of the lifting of sanctions, following implementation of the nuclear deal.[33] Iran may use the anticipated windfall once sanctions are lifted to make a number of major conventional arms purchases.[34] Nonetheless, nuclear weapons are ultimately the most cost-effective way for Iran to consolidate its status as the dominant regional power; while a nuclear weapons program might cost tens of billions of dollars, rebuilding its conventional military could cost Iran hundreds of billions of dollars.

The IRI's pursuit of status and influence also manifests itself in frequent demands for reciprocity in its relations with the outside world—and in particular, with great powers such as the United States. Iran insists that peaceful interactions with other countries be based on "mutual respect" while it has often declared that, in response to hostile acts, it will match "threat with threat" and respond proportionally and in kind (see below).[35]

Deterrence and Defense. Iranian defense planning is also motivated by a desire to enhance the IRI's deterrent capability. To this end, Iran has created a force tailored to deter the countries that it believes pose the greatest threat to it. Its deterrent "red lines" likely include: 1) direct attacks on Iran; 2) measures to close down its ability to export oil; 3) threats to its territorial integrity; 4) overt attempts at regime change, and; 5) the return of major US ground combat units to Iraq.

Iran has a declaratory policy of deterrence by punishment as well as denial. Thus, it has threatened to respond to an American and/or Israeli preventive strike on Iran with a "crushing response,"[36] by destroying the Israeli cities of Tel Aviv and Haifa,[37] and by launching missiles strikes against US bases throughout the region.[38] It has vowed that any attack on Iran would result in the defeat of the enemy's designs.[39] And it has created a "Passive Defense Organization" to harden and disperse critical infrastructure, to limit the benefits an adversary might accrue from striking them.

Threat Perceptions. Supreme Leader Ali Khamenei and many around him believe that Iran has been at war with its neighbors and the West since the early days of the Islamic Revolution. At various times, the Islamic Republic has faced perceived and real external threats from Iraq, the United States, Israel, Afghanistan, and Saudi Arabia. These have come mainly from the west (Iraq and Israel), the south (US naval forces in the Gulf), and to a lesser extent from the east (the Taliban in Afghanistan). Tehran has in the past also feared perceived American attempts to encircle it—an apprehension fed by US military campaigns in neighboring Afghanistan and Iraq—as well as threats of subversion by the United States (in the form of 'soft warfare') and Saudi Arabia (through its support for Sunni opposition groups).

Iranian force dispositions have traditionally reflected these deep-seated threat perceptions, with most of Iran's ground forces based near the border with Iraq, most of its air force based near Iraq and the Persian Gulf region, and its main missile silo fields located in the northwest and western regions of the country. Its navy is almost exclusively deployed in the Gulf, though Iran aspires to build a blue water navy capable of mounting a forward defense, projecting Iranian influence, and showing the flag around the world.[40]

The IRI still considers the United States—the "Great Satan" and quintessential embodiment of the forces of "global arrogance"—as its principal enemy and the main threat to its interests and survival.[41] According to senior Iranian military officials, the nature of the threat posed by the United States has passed through several phases:[42]

- The US initially sought the overthrow of the Islamic Republic by proxy—by supporting the Iraqi invasion of Iran in 1980;

- When that failed, it invaded Afghanistan and Iraq, to pave the way for the invasion of Iran and the overthrow of the IRI—though these efforts were thwarted when the US became mired in insurgencies in both countries;

- Following the failure of these military efforts, the US purportedly attempted to undermine the IRI by soft warfare, in order to foment a color revolution in Iran—the 2009 "sedition" (i.e. the Green Movement)—which was ultimately quashed by the regime;

- The US then tried to destroy the "axis of resistance" by fomenting a civil war in Syria, which was defeated due to the intervention of Hizballah, Iran, and their allies;

- With the failure of its previous "hard" and "soft" warfare efforts, the US then tried to undermine Iran through cyber warfare and sanctions.

Iran's "Deterrent Triad." To deal with the array of threats it faces, the IRI has sought to bolster its defense and war-fighting capabilities by creating a deterrent triad that rests on its ability to: 1) undertake subversion and terror on several continents; 2) threaten the flow of oil through the Strait of Hormuz, and; 3) launch long-range strikes, primarily by missiles (though Iran has also endowed some of its proxies and partners, like Hizballah and Hamas, with rockets that provide similar capabilities against Israel). To this end, Iran has

Michael Eisenstadt

devoted the lion's share of its limited defense dollars in past decades to enhancing its proxy and unconventional warfare forces, creating a guerilla navy, and expanding its rocket and missile forces, to enable it to land a "crushing blow" against its enemies if deterrence fails.[43]

Proxy and Unconventional Warfare Forces. The IRI has long relied on armed proxies and partners to project influence abroad. These include groups such as the Lebanese Hizballah and Iraqi Shi'ite militias and "special groups" such as the Badr organization, Asaib Ahl-al-Haqq, and Kataib Hizballah. More recently it has added to its roster of proxies many of the numerous Iraqi "Popular Mobilization Units" created after the fall of Mosul to IS in June 2014, Syria's so-called "National Defense Forces," and even recently formed Afghan and Pakistani Shi'ites militias which have fought in Syria under its aegis. Iran has also supported Hamas and Palestinian Islamic Jihad in the Palestinian arena. The IRGC's Qods Force is the entity responsible for training and employing these forces.

Some of these proxies and partners have been innovators in the field of unconventional warfare: Hizballah pioneered the use of suicide bombing and of battlefield rockets as strategic bombardment systems against Israel, Hamas conducted suicide bombing campaigns and pioneered the use of homemade rockets, also against Israel, while Shi'ite 'special groups' in Iraq used Explosively Formed Projectiles (EFPs) and Improvised Rocket-Assisted Munitions (IRAMs) against US forces there. These groups have greatly enhanced Tehran's ability to project influence in the region, and are part and parcel of its deterrent complex; if Israel or the United States were to attack Iran's nuclear infrastructure, Iran would likely rely on Hizballah, and perhaps some of its other proxies to respond.[44]

Guerilla Navy. Iran has built a navy capable of waging asymmetric naval guerilla warfare as part of its anti-access strategy in the Gulf. Regular and IRGC-Navy forces would employ swarm tactics, mines, anti-ship missiles, small boats, midget and conventional submarines, combat swimmers, and rockets and missiles, to disrupt shipping in the Gulf and control passage through the Strait of Hormuz.[45] Iran is also building a blue water navy to enable it to mount a forward defense outside the Gulf, and inflict casualties on enemy naval forces long before they attempt to pass through the Strait.[46]

Strategic Rocket and Missile Forces. Iran has the largest missile force in the Middle East, producing long-range rockets, short- and medium-range ballistic missiles, and long-range cruise missiles. All of these are believed to be conventionally armed. Due to their poor accuracy, they would probably be used as weapons of mass terror against enemy cities. Iran's medium-range ballistic missiles could also deliver a first-generation nuclear weapon.[47]

Numerous cities in Iraq and along the shores of the Persian Gulf are well within the range of Iran's most capable rocket systems, some with a claimed range of 500km. Iran is also believed to have 800-1,000 short- and medium-range ballistic missiles; some of the latter have a claimed range of more than 2,000km— sufficient to reach targets throughout the Gulf, Israel, and southeastern Europe. Iran has built a large rocket and missile force to overwhelm enemy rocket and missile defenses, ensuring a dramatic psychological impact on the enemy.

The IRI's efforts to create a massive conventional strategic bombardment capability is a lesson of the Iran-Iraq War, when conventional missile strikes on Tehran during the 1988 War of the Cities led to the evacuation of a quarter of the city's residents. This contributed to the demoralization of the Iranian public and, ultimately, to the decision to bring the war to an end.[48]

Iranian rockets are, moreover, central to the "way of war" of Iranian proxies and allies such as Hizballah and Hamas. The manner in which both Hezbollah and Hamas used rockets in their recent wars with Israel provides a useful template for understanding the role of conventionally armed missiles in Iran's warfighting doctrine. And as terror weapons, rockets and missiles are equally effective; civilians are indifferent to whether they are being targeted by unguided or guided systems.

However, not all three legs of Iran's deterrent/warfighting triad are equally useful. Closing the Strait could have a major impact on the world economy, but would be a last resort for Tehran—it's "Sampson Option"—

because nearly all of Iran's own oil exports go through the strait, and closing it would alienate much of the international community. At any rate, Iran lacks the ability to keep the strait closed for a significant amount of time.[49]

While terrorist attacks afford a degree of standoff and deniability, Iran's ability to wage terror has atrophied in recent years, as demonstrated by the bungled attacks on Israeli diplomatic targets in Europe and Asia in February 2012.[50] Moreover, during a protracted crisis or war, Iran may need weeks to organize follow-on terrorist attacks, which may not succeed against an alerted enemy. However, its recent creation of a "foreign legion" comprised of not just Lebanese, but Syrian, Iraqi, Afghan, and Pakistani Shi'ite militias, may expand its future options in this area.

For all these reasons, Iran's missile force will remain the backbone of its strategic deterrent. Missiles afford a quicker, more flexible response during a rapidly moving crisis, and when launched in large numbers, can saturate enemy defenses and generate greater cumulative effects in a shorter period of time than can terrorist attacks.[51] And in the future, Iran may try to develop nontraditional delivery means for conventional and nonconventional payloads, such as special forces, unmanned aerial vehicles, and boats.

People's War. Iran fears dismemberment, foreign meddling, and invasion. In the distant past, Iran was invaded and occupied by Macedonians, Arabs, and Mongols. In the early 19 ʰ century it was forced to cede territory to Russia. During World War II, it was occupied by the UK and USSR. In 1953, the US and Britain conspired to overthrow Iran's duly elected Prime Minister, Mohammad Mosaddeq. And it feared invasion after the failed 1980 US hostage rescue and the 2003 US intervention in Iraq.

In April 1980, the IRI created the Basij, a popular militia auxiliary intended to be a "20 million man army" (the actual number is believed to be perhaps 4-5 million)[52] which is controlled by the IRGC. The primary mission of the Basij is internal security, and waging a "popular war" against an invader.[53] Iran has tried to create similar popular militias in Iraq and Syria, in an effort to remake its allies in its own image.

After the 2003 US invasion of Iraq, Iran sought to elevate people's war to a fourth leg of its deterrent complex: the Basij and IRGC were trained to conduct guerilla warfare against an invader in accordance with a new, decentralized defensive concept—the regime's so-called "mosaic" doctrine.[54]

However, once the US became mired in costly counterinsurgency campaigns in Iraq and Afghanistan, and as the threat of invasion faded, the IRI increasingly focused on the perceived threat of a "soft" revolution fomented by the United States.[55]

Cyber. Most recently, the IRI has been developing its cyber capability into what may eventually become a fourth leg of its deterrent complex. The potential to cause great harm to the critical infrastructure of its enemies, while maintaining a degree of deniability, likely makes cyber a very appealing option for Iran.[56]

Supporting Activities. In addition to strengthening deterrence by building up its military capabilities, Iran has taken steps to bolster its deterrent image and posture through a variety of non-military supporting activities:

- Nurturing a culture of resistance, jihad, and martyrdom in order to strengthen its staying power and intimidate its enemies;

- Building oil and gas pipelines with its neighbors (such as the so-called peace pipeline that will link Iran and Pakistan, if it is ever finished) and tying neighboring states into its electrical grid (Iran provides Iraq with 5-10 percent of its electricity). In addition to the economic benefits and political leverage such arrangements confer (similar to the leverage that the EU's dependence on Russian gas confers on Moscow), Tehran apparently hopes that these dependencies will ensure that its neighbors have an incentive to press the United States to not attack Iran;[57]

- Establishing ties with Shi'ite and Muslim communities worldwide, by co-opting Shi'ite clerical networks and engaging in religious outreach via Iranian cultural centers, which are often staffed by intelligence personnel. Iran may hope that these ties will induce these communities to rally to its side if it is attacked;

- Hardening and dispersing its nuclear facilities and other critical infrastructure to make them less vulnerable, thereby deterring enemies by denying them lucrative targets;

- Participating in nuclear negotiations with the P5+1/EU as an insurance policy, since they are presumably safe from attack as long as diplomacy is a viable option.

Ambiguity. Iran has frequently used ambiguity to bolster deterrence. Thus, since 2006, Iranian officials have repeatedly declared that Iran is a "nuclear power," using this term in a way that plays on its multiple meanings.[58] Likewise, the Supreme Leader has issued a "non-denial denial" of nuclear intent, declaring that "We believe that nuclear weapons must be eliminated. We don't want to build atomic weapons. But if we didn't believe so and intended to possess nuclear weapons, no power could stop us."[59] Iran has used displays of its missile forces in parades and exercises to play on the perceived connection between missiles and nuclear weapons, which it has encouraged by decorating the missiles with banners proclaiming "Death to America" and "Israel should be wiped off the map."[60]

Tehran's policy of nuclear ambiguity also potentially complicates US efforts to establish a regional security architecture to deter and contain an Iran that is a nuclear threshold state. As demonstrated by the firestorm that greeted then Secretary of State Hillary Clinton's July 2009 statement regarding a US "defense umbrella" for the region, such declarations could lead friends and allies to believe that Washington has reconciled itself to Iran's eventual acquisition of nuclear weapons, thereby advancing Tehran's goal of being treated as a latent nuclear weapons state.[61]

Preemption. In response to Israeli and US threats of preventive military action against its nuclear program, Iran has supplemented its policy of deterrence with its own doctrine of preemption. Thus, in comments published in September 2012, IRGC Aerospace Force commander Brigadier General Amir Ali Hajizadeh stated that

> Starting wars and aggression does not exist in the strategy of the Islamic Republic of Iran... However, under conditions when [our enemies] have prepared everything for war, it is possible that we will engage in preemptive attacks. I do not dismiss this, but now, I do not see the tactical and operational issues in the region in such a way that they, for example, would want to attack us tomorrow. [But] If we find out that they are ready and want to attack us, we will not allow our forces to be surprised...[62]

Self-Reliance. Since its inception, the IRI has been a "strategically lonely" state, lacking reliable allies or a superpower patron. This reflects, in part, Iran's status as a predominantly Shi'ite-Persian state in a region dominated by Sunni Arabs and Turks, and the legacy of radical policies that have alienated neighbors and isolated it internationally.

Thus, during the Iran-Iraq War, Tehran faced Baghdad virtually alone. A US-led arms embargo greatly complicated Iran's efforts to sustain its war effort, and Iran's sense of isolation and abandonment was heightened by the apathetic international response to Iraq's use of chemical weapons in that war. This experience has left deep wounds in the Iranian national psyche, and inculcated a profound distrust of international arms control treaties as well as some international organizations (such as the International Atomic Energy Agency (IAEA)) and some UN bodies (such as the Security Council). And it has bred a determination in Iran that these bitter experiences not be repeated.

As a result, Iran sought to develop its own military industries and to create a nuclear option in order to reduce its dependence on foreign arms suppliers, minimize the impact of future embargoes, and create the foundation for a modern military.

The pursuit of self-reliance—a central element of the IRI's revolutionary ethos that extends to all spheres of national life—reflects a determination to free Iran of the dependence on foreign technology and advisors that characterized the Shah's efforts to modernize and transform the country. As a result of more than thirty-five years of exertions, the IRI has become less dependent on foreign suppliers for advanced arms, equipment, and technology. And while it remains dependent on foreign suppliers for special materials and certain technologies, it downplays or denies outright this dependence, and often exaggerates its achievements in this domain.[63]

SOFT POWER

The IRI has traditionally pursued a mixed soft/hard power national security strategy that prioritized soft power over hard power. This is because its leaders believe in the primacy of the moral, spiritual, and psychological dimensions of statecraft and strategy, and not because it is a failed hard power "wannabe."[64] Likewise, Iran's apparent decision to eschew a large, balanced conventional force structure may reflect an approach to national security that places greater emphasis on guile than on brute force,[65] and on soft power than on hard power.[66]

The IRI's leaders believe that US "soft warfare" (in effect, the "weaponization" of American soft power) has the potential to alienate Iran's youth from the ideology of the revolution, undermine popular support for the regime, and sap the social cohesion of the IRI. They fear that this loss of commitment, cohesion, and faith will not only doom the Islamic Republic to failure in this world, but condemn the souls of believers to perdition in the world to come. Thus, according to hard-line Assembly of Experts member Ayatollah Mohammad Taghi Mesbah Yazdi, "If we are defeated in hard warfare, the afterlife reward will be awaiting us, but defeat in soft warfare means losing worldly and afterlife salvation." [67]

Conversely, US officials tend to be wedded to a hard power approach to strategy and statecraft that under-plays the importance of soft power. Thus, in assessing the threat posed by Tehran, US military planners and policymakers tend to focus on Iran's hard power assets—particularly its unconventional warfare and naval anti-access capabilities, its rocket and missile forces, and its nuclear program. This reflects an American preoccupation with capabilities that can produce physical effects, rooted in a certain conception of military power.

During the final phases of the US occupation of Iraq, US officials fretted that the Iraqi military would be unprepared to secure the country's airspace and waters against Iranian military incursions after US forces left, while it was Iran's political influence, its influence over Iraqi militias, and its economic, religious, and informational activities that posed, and continued to pose, the greater long-term threat to Iraqi sovereignty and independence. US officials tend to overlook or misunderstand the key role that soft power—and particularly propaganda and psychological warfare—plays in Iran's defense and foreign policies.[68]

For Iran, soft power encompasses the non-military elements of national power, and includes the following:

Reputation and image management: Tehran presents itself as a dependable partner, a formidable adversary, as well as a moral force in the world, and it pushes a triumphalist narrative that asserts that it is a rising power that has God and history on its side. Its recent successes in extending its influence in Syria, Iraq, and Yemen have enhanced its image and standing in the region among its supporters, while unnerving its adversaries. Its spin has often been undercut, however, by its own political and economic problems and by the tendency of Iranian officials to issue vain and provocative boasts, to meddle in their neighbors' affairs, to over-promise and under-deliver on aid commitments, and to lecture and condescend toward others (particularly Arabs).

Thus, in a March 2015 speech, Iranian presidential advisor and former Intelligence Minister Ali Younesi proclaimed that Iran was a new empire with a sphere of influence spanning from China to the Persian Gulf, adding that "Currently, Iraq is not only part of our civilisational influence, but it is our identity, culture, centre and capital…Because Iran and Iraq's geography and culture are inseparable, either we fight one another or we become one."[69] This provoked a backlash in Iraq, from not only Sunnis, but Shi'ites as well, with Grand Ayatollah Ali Sistani's representative stating in response that "we are proud of our country and our identity and our independence and sovereignty."[70]

IRGC Qods Force commander Qasem Soleimani has likewise alienated many Iraqis with his high-profile role in the campaign by Iraqi Shi'ite militias against IS following the fall of Mosul, and his efforts to block political reforms sponsored by Iraqi Prime Minister Haidar al-Abadi that could diminish the clout of some of Tehran's closest Iraqi allies, including former Prime Minister Nuri al-Maliki.[71]

Export of revolutionary Islam: During the first decade after the Islamic Revolution, Iran invested significant efforts in exporting its revolution elsewhere in the Middle East by various means, including coup attempts (Bahrain in 1981), the creation of militia proxies (the Lebanese Hizballah in 1982), and attempted assassinations (Kuwait in 1985). It built up the Lebanese Hizballah as a partner and proxy in prosecuting its struggle against the enemies of the IRI, and spreading its ideology to Shi'ite communities throughout the region and beyond.

Since then, wherever there have been embattled Shi'ite communities and weak states in the Middle East, Iran has tried to create militia proxies to expand its influence. And where these militias can be found, one can also find Iran's culture of resistance, jihad, and martyrdom being propagated as a first step toward institutionalizing Iranian influence in those societies, with participation in politics as the next step. Thus, Hizballah parlayed its military achievements as a resistance organization (and the goodwill engendered by its social-welfare activities) into political capital, transforming itself into a political party with a blocking vote in the Lebanese government. Several Iraqi Hizballah clones have tried to do the same, though without the same degree of success thus far.

The Arab uprisings, the Syrian civil war, and the rise of IS have created new opportunities for Iran to export its revolutionary ideology and expand its influence. Thus, the IRI has taken first steps toward remaking the region in its own image by creating popular militias in Iraq (the so-called Popular Mobilization Forces)[72] and Syria (the National Defense Forces),[73] drawing largely on local Shi'ite communities and Shi'ite foreign fighters of Afghan and Pakistani origin.[74]

By doing so, Iran has broadened and strengthened its regional alliance system—the so-called "axis of resistance," and broadened and deepened its array of contacts in these societies. Iran's creation of a transnational Shi'ite network consisting of Syrians, Iraqis, Afghans, and Pakistanis, will create future opportunities for it to project its influence throughout the region and beyond.[75] The IRI's proxy militias show how its soft and hard power often go hand-in-hand.

Tehran has also sought to ensure the primacy of its brand of revolutionary Islam in Shi'ite communities around the world by spending large sums of money to support the activities of clerics trained in Qom and steeped in the ideology of clerical rule, and by co-opting or displacing clerics trained elsewhere (such as Najaf).[76] In the words of President Hassan Rouhani, "the West's mistake is that it thinks that the Islamic Republic is seeking an opportunity for military dominance in the region, while we are not pursuing it. Our strength is our thought's dominance in the entire region."[77] Tehran also seeks to create bonds of religious solidarity with Shi'ite communities around the world that can serve as external bases of support for its policies and as allies should it be attacked.[78]

Economic leverage: Tehran pursues trade and investment with other countries for profit, and to foster dependencies which it can exploit. In Iraq, for instance, it has used business deals to bolster local allies, and it has dumped cheap, subsidized produce and consumer goods on the local market, undercutting Iraq's agricultural and manufacturing sectors. Moreover, Iraq's reliance on Iran for some of its electricity needs is a dependency which many Iraqis believe that Tehran manipulates for political ends; for instance, in June 2010, Iran reportedly cut electricity supplies to Basra to bolster Sadrist claims that the government was lagging in the delivery of services.[79]

Propaganda and spin: Iran vies for Arab "hearts and minds" through Arabic-language news broadcasts that reflect Tehran's propaganda line. These efforts have generally come up short, however, due to maladroit implementation, the IRI's tendency to be its own worst enemy in its dealings with its Arab neighbors, and actions that often undercut its messaging.[80] Past polling data has generally shown that Arabs (including Iraqi Shi'ite Arabs) distrust Iran and do not considered its form of governance a viable model.[81] These negative attitudes explain why Tehran has in the past leaned heavily on soft power, its intelligence services, and covert action to project influence in the Arab world.

This, however, may be changing, as a result of Iran's efforts to forge a transnational Shi'ite network to counter the transnational Sunni networks created by salafi-jihadist groups like IS and al-Qaeda. With the sectarian polarization of the region, Iran may find more willing allies among embattled Shi'ite communities in Iraq and elsewhere than in the past, and more enemies among the region's Sunnis than ever before. And its involvement in ongoing conflicts in Syria and Iraq has forced Iran to rely more heavily than ever before on hard power and overt military intervention to prop up its regional allies—though its willingness to do so has enhance its stature in their eyes.

A responsible global citizen: Iran has also tried to bolster its soft power by presenting itself as a responsible global citizen by virtue, *inter alia*, of its status as a signatory to the Chemical Weapons Convention (CWC), the Biological Weapons Convention (BWC), and the Nuclear Nonproliferation Treaty (NPT), as well as Ayatollah Khamenei's nuclear *fatwa*, which bans the development, stockpiling, and use of nuclear weapons.[82] Iran has generally made a show of ostensibly observing its legal obligations at declared and safeguarded nuclear facilities, such as the power plant at Bushehr, in order to bolster these claims—though it is also the only country in the world operating a nuclear power plant that has not signed onto the international Convention on Nuclear Safety.

While professedly embracing its nonproliferation commitments under these agreements, Iran has in the past displayed an ambivalent attitude toward arms control treaties. Iran's traumatic experience as a victim of chemical warfare during the Iran-Iraq War has caused many senior officials to be skeptical of international law and treaties. Thus, in 1988, then Majles speaker and acting commander-in-chief of the armed forces, Ali Akbar Hashemi Rafsanjani stated in a speech to military officers, that

> Chemical and biological weapons are poor man's atomic bombs and can easily be produced. We should at least consider them for our defense. Although the use of such weapons is inhuman, the [Iran-Iraq] war taught us that international laws are only scraps of paper.[83]

Despite these misgivings, Iran goes to great lengths to emphasize its participation in and adherence to all of the aforementioned major arms control treaties—even though it is not clear that it is in compliance with its obligations under the CWC,[84] and it has a long record of engaging in undeclared nuclear activities in violation of its IAEA, and possibly NPT obligations.[85] For instance, Iran has:

- Engaged in the undeclared and illicit procurement of sensitive nuclear-relevant technologies since the mid-1980s—activities that continue to this day;[86]

- Conducted undeclared experiments related to centrifuge and laser enrichment and the separation of plutonium, and attempted to build undeclared facilities capable of producing fissile material at Natanz and Arak (revealed in 2002) and at Fordow (revealed in 2009);[87]

- Engaged in weapons-related research-and-development work prior to 2003, and perhaps after, and refused to clarify concerns regarding possible military dimensions of its nuclear program.[88]

Likewise, for more than a decade Iran has denied the IAEA access to personnel, documents, and sites or facilities needed to resolve questions related to possible military dimensions of its program, and it has rejected the legality of and ignored a half-dozen Security Council resolutions passed since 2006 that, *inter alia*, required it to suspend enrichment- and reprocessing-related activities.[89]

Michael Eisenstadt

Tehran has also tried to present itself as a credible partner of the international community in the fight against IS in Syria and Iraq, even though Iran's policies and those of its allies helped foster the group's rise and its continued success. Tehran's principal regional ally—Syria's Bashar al-Asad—was complicit in the rise of IS: he allowed al-Qaeda in Iraq (which later became IS) to use Syria's territory to stage operations in Iraq during the US occupation, and since 2011 he allowed IS to consolidate control over parts of eastern Syria so that he could portray IS as an imminent threat to his regime, while presenting his regime as a partner in the fight against it. And in Iraq, Shi'ite militias supported by Tehran have engaged in extrajudicial killings of Sunni Arabs and the wholesale destruction of Sunni communities, thereby reinforcing Islamic State's appeal among this sector of the population.[90]

Toward a Rebalanced Soft/Hard Power Strategy? While Iran has traditionally emphasized soft power, it has not ignored its 'hard power' assets, as indicated by its proxy warfare capabilities, its guerilla navy, its robust missile force, and its nuclear program. Iran's recent military interventions in Syria and Iraq have, moreover, highlighted the essential importance of hard power in certain situations. Iran has for the first time committed advisors in large numbers (some of whom have served in combat roles), as well as small numbers of combat pilots and IRGC ground troops to assist Syria and Iraq in their fight against IS.[91] As a result, Iran may be rethinking the relative weight of soft and hard power, (and of indirect and direct approaches to the use of force) in its foreign and defense policies, though casualty figures show that Iran is still trying to minimize its exposure in Syria and Iraq, and that it continues to lean heavily on its proxies and allies whenever possible.[92] Indeed, had Iran been willing to commit more of its own forces earlier on, Syrian forces might not have required Russian intervention to survive.

Looking toward the more distant future, nuclear weapons could provide the IRI with the status and hard power attributes commensurate to its grandiose ambitions, while serving as the ultimate soft power enabler for Tehran—demonstrating how the IRI's soft and hard power are two sides of the same coin.

THE IRI'S "WAY OF WAR"

Tehran's approach to dealing with its adversaries has been shaped by a number of principles that have long guided Iranian policy, and that together comprise the IRI's "way of war." These include: 1) the use of indirection (proxies), ambiguity (deniability and standoff), and strategic patience, in order to manage risk; 2) reciprocity, proportionality, and the calibrated use of violence; 3) emphasis on the moral, spiritual, and psychological dimensions of statecraft and strategy; 4) tactical flexibility, and; 5) efforts to disaggregate hostile coalitions by driving wedges between adversaries.

Indirection, Ambiguity, and Strategic Patience. Tehran prefers to avoid head-on confrontations and instead to deal with adversaries by indirect means (such as proxies) or unconventional methods, sometimes far removed in space and time from prior rounds of conflict. It does so, at least in part, to manage risk and thereby reduce the potential for escalation. And it seeks to achieve its goals and to prevail over its adversaries through incremental steps and small victories, rather than rapid progress and decisive victories (America's preferred "way of war").

Thus, during the Iran-Iraq War, Iran countered US convoy operations with covertly sown minefields, Silkworm missile attacks that skirted US "red lines," and small-boat attacks against unescorted vessels; it has often relied on proxies, such as the Lebanese Hizballah, to strike at its enemies in the Middle East, Europe, South America, and Asia; and it tried to avoid rousing international opposition to its nuclear program (for many years, successfully) by making slow, incremental progress, and engaging in what some have called a "slow motion nuclear breakout."[93]

Proxy Warfare. The use of street mobs and violent pressure groups as instruments of domestic politics is an old tradition in Iran, going back at least to the Qajar dynasty.[94] Thus, regime sponsored vigilantes (such as the thugs of Ansar-e Hizballah) played a key role in repressing domestic unrest in Iran in 1999 and 2009. This form of domestic politics "by other means" finds its corollary in Iran's use of militia and terrorist surrogates as an instrument of foreign policy. Iran's proxy operations are thus an external manifestation of its approach to domestic politics and conflict.

For Tehran, reliance on proxies is not a "weapon of the weak," but a preferred *modus operandi* that is central to its way of war.[95] After all, if one believes that one's enemies are constantly conspiring and working through agents and proxies, one is also more likely to act in a conspiratorial fashion and to operate through agents and proxies. And reliance on proxies is a way for Tehran to manage risk vis-à-vis its adversaries.

These proxies allow the IRI to shape regional dynamics and project influence far from its borders. Hizballah in particular plays a critical role in Iran's deterrence posture, and would play a major role in any retaliation for a US or Israeli strike against Iran. Reliance on proxies also provides plausible deniability and complicates retaliation by its enemies—although standoff is more important for Tehran than deniability, as it is not always careful to cover its tracks.[96]

Whenever possible, Tehran will fight to its last Arab proxy, rather than commit its own military to combat. When Iran has wanted to strike out at its enemies, it has often commissioned or enabled operations by these proxies, and when it has served Tehran's purposes, it has helped proxies to conduct their own operations. Thus:

• In an apparent attempt to eject the United States from the Middle East, the IRI facilitated the October 23, 1983 Marine barracks bombing by Hizballah's Islamic Jihad Organization that killed 241 Marines, and led to the withdrawal of US forces from Lebanon.[97]

• In response to the targeted killing of Hizballah secretary general Sheikh Abbas Musawi by Israeli forces on February 16, 1992, Hizballah, with assistance from Iran's Ministry of Intelligence and Security, bombed the Israeli embassy in Buenos Aires on May 19, 1992.[98]

• In response to an Israeli air strike on a training base in Ayn Dardara, Lebanon on June 2, 1994, which killed dozens of Hizballah recruits and IRGC trainers, Hizballah (with Iran's help) bombed a Jewish community center in Buenos Aires on July 18, 1994, killing 85 and wounding hundreds.[99]

• After Congress authorized $18-20 million for covert operations in Iran, IRGC-QF and Lebanese Hizballah commissioned Saudi Hizballah to bomb a US military housing complex in Dharan, Saudi Arabia, on June 25, 1996, killing 19 US service members and wounding 372 others.[100]

• After Saudi forces helped Bahrain quash protests by largely Shi'ite opposition groups in March 2011, Iran is believed to have launched a series of attacks on Saudi diplomats in Pakistan and Egypt, and it attempted to recruit a Mexican narco-terrorist to assassinate the Saudi ambassador in Washington, DC.[101]

Iran's proxy operations are conducted in accordance with a well-worn playbook. Iran will often peel off extremists from established, mainstream Shi'ite groups it has ties to, in order to create radical proxies. It did this in Lebanon when it recruited more extreme members of the moderate Amal party to create the Hizballah movement in the early 1980s, and in Iraq in the past decade when it splintered off members from the Badr organization, such as Abu Mustafa al-Sheibani and Abu Mahdi al-Muhandis, as well as members of Muqtada al-Sadr's Mahdi Army militia, such as Qais al-Khazali and Ismail al-Lami (a.k.a. Abu Dira'—the notorious "Shi'ite Zarqawi"), to form covert special groups.[102]

Tehran is also tactically flexible (more on this later), and not exclusively monogamous, and its use of proxies has been guided largely by opportunistic and pragmatic, rather than ideological considerations. Thus, it has supported a variety of militias and insurgent groups in Iraq, at times backing nearly every horse in the race—since one is bound to win. It has supported Shi'ite militias such as the Badr Corps (later renamed the Badr Organization), the Mahdi Army, Asaib Ahl al-Haqq, and Kataib Hizballah, while also backing the government of Iraq—though the former have sometimes fought among themselves, and have often acted to undermine the authority of the latter.

Iran has supported not just Shi'ites; it has also supported Sunni groups such as the Palestinian Islamic Jihad and Hamas (though the former is the rare Sunni group that subscribes to the IRI's ideology). Tehran has even shown a willingness at times to strike temporary tactical alliances with its strategic enemies, working with Sunni salafi-jihadist groups such as Ansar al-Islam—in order to gain leverage over its erstwhile Kurdish allies, and with al-Qaeda in Iraq during the US occupation—in order to keep sectarian violence at a roil and to bloody US forces there.[103]

There are, however, disadvantages to relying on proxies over which it does not always have full control. Thus, in 2006, Hizballah stumbled into a war with Israel that led to the destruction of Hizballah's long-range rocket forces—a key element of Iran's strategic deterrent. And in 2007, Iranian-sponsored Iraqi Shi'ite militias engaged in internecine violence and acted in ways that undercut the authority of the Iranian-supported central government, contributing to the latter's 2008 decision to crack down on the Mahdi Army and Shi'ite special groups.[104] In both of these cases, Tehran's proxies and allies acted in ways that harmed Iran's image and interests.

There are also questions as to how much Tehran can rely on even its closest allies in a crunch. In 2012, Hizballah leader Hassan Nasrallah indicated that in the event of an Israeli preventive strike, the decision on whether to retaliate would be Hizballah's alone to make:

> Concerning future events in the region, there is this analysis that what would happen should Israel target Iran's nuclear installations. I tell you this: On that day, which I think is unlikely to happen, the Iranian leadership will not demand anything from Hizballah... But I stress that on that day it is us who will sit, think and decide what to do... [105]

Several months later—almost certainly after receiving a private rebuke from Iran—Nasrallah stated that in the event of an Israeli strike, "a decision has [already] been taken to respond and the response will be very great."[106] In such a scenario, Hizballah would likely be torn between its obligation to assist its Iranian patron and partner in "resistance," and its desire to avoid actions that could harm its standing with its Lebanese supporters. Hizballah's ongoing military involvement in Syria and Yemen will only heighten this dilemma.

In the end, the obligations flowing from Hizballah's adherence to the doctrine of clerical rule (or guardianship of the jurist—*velayet-e faqih*) require Nasrallah and Hizballah to yield to Supreme Leader Khamenei's will, though the latter, undoubtedly aware of Hizballah's domestic political constraints, and in accordance with the doctrine of expediency, would likely not demand of Hizballah more than it can afford (politically) to deliver.[107]

Not all of Tehran's allies identify closely with the IRI. Hamas became an ally of Iran in the 1990s by default, for lack of a better alternative, and not because of any ideological affinity with the Islamic Republic. (Likewise, the Shi'ite Houthis in Yemen do not accept the doctrine of clerical rule, even if they are glad to accept Iranian military assistance.)

Accordingly, when Hamas leader Khalid Mashal was asked during a February 2006 visit to Tehran University how Hamas would respond if Israel attacked Iran, he responded "Have no fear, we will pray for you," adding, with a an uneasy laugh, when an Iranian student retorted that Israel would be destroyed if it attacked Iran, "if you destroy Israel, you will be doing so over our heads."[108] And with the onset of the Syrian civil war in 2011, Hamas supported those seeking to overthrow Bashar al-Asad, Tehran's foremost Arab ally, leading to a chill in relations that has continued to this day.

Paradoxically, because Tehran makes so much of its support for members of the "axis of resistance", such as Hizballah and Hamas, and because it has often basked in the reflected glory of their military achievements, it is partially dependent on these proxies and partners for its domestic legitimacy and regional standing, and cannot be seen as abandoning them in time of need. In particular, its differences with Hamas in recent years over Syria have been a source of embarrassment. In many ways, Tehran needs these groups—politically and militarily—as much as they need Iran.

Neither is Tehran always a reliable partner. It has repeatedly abandoned embattled Shi'ite communities to their fate (as stated previously) and withheld aid from allies and proxies, when its interests dictated that it do so:

- During the 2006 Lebanon War and the 2008-2009 and 2012 Wars in Gaza, Iran neither intervened on behalf of its allies nor permitted Iranian volunteers to leave for the front.[109]

- Iran reneged on its commitment to send an aid flotilla to Gaza in 2010 (after a Turkish NGO had previously done so).[110]

- After Ali Akbar Velayati, senior advisor to Ali Khamenei, warned Israel in January 2013 that an attack on Syria would be considered an attack on Iran, the latter did nothing in the face of nearly a dozen subsequent Israeli attacks in Syria on convoys carrying weapons for Hizballah.[111]

- And when Syria reportedly asked Iran to retaliate against Israel in response to an Israeli strike in February 2013, Iran reportedly refused to do so.[112]

- Likewise, Hizballah refused requests from Hamas to join the fight against Israel during the 2008-2009 Gaza War, and again during the 2014 Gaza War.[113]

It is not always easy to be an ally of Iran or Hizballah.

Strategic Patience. In accordance with its preference for avoiding decisive engagements and head-on confrontations, the IRI has repeatedly demonstrated a preference for "Fabian" strategies of delay, indirection, and attrition.[114]Thus, the Islamic Republic has:

- Drawn out its nuclear negotiations with the EU and then the P5+1 to buy time for its program, enabling it to make slow, incremental progress in the interim;[115]

- Intimidated, demoralized, and worn down the domestic opposition by holding show trials of opposition leaders, conducting mass arrests, and torturing and maltreating detainees;

- Tried to ensnare Israel in a wearying, demoralizing, open-ended conflict with Lebanese Hizballah and Palestinian Hamas;

- Been careful to take on the US only by indirect means, relying on surrogates such as the Lebanese Hizballah and Iraqi 'special groups.'

Tehran has often taken months to retaliate for perceived acts of aggression, to ensure it takes place at a time and place of its choosing. Thus, some six months after the US Congress authorized funds for covert operations to destabilize Iran, Saudi Hizballah carried out the June 1996 Khobar Towers bombing in Saudi Arabia.[116] Likewise, some six months after Saudi forces helped Bahrain to quash popular unrest in that Gulf kingdom in March 2011, US law enforcement thwarted a plot to assassinate the Saudi ambassador in Washington.

This preference for strategies of indirection and attrition is well-suited to a culture that operates on an extended time horizon,[117] and whose senior political and military leadership is characterized by a great deal of continuity. (Many senior government officials have filled key positions since the early 1980s, and Iran's election cycle does not affect those positions that have the greatest influence on foreign and defense policy—most notably that of Supreme Leader.) It is an alien way of thinking, however, for impatient Americans whose contemporary popular culture emphasizes instant gratification in the form of "fast food," "instant messaging," and "overnight delivery;" whose strategic culture emphasizes "surges," "decisive operations," and "exit strategies;" and whose political culture is shaped by a twenty-four hour news cycle and a four year electoral cycle (which gives a sitting president only two-and-a-half years to focus on his policy agenda before her focus turns to reelection).

Iranians can look to Islamic and Iranian history for examples of the benefits of forbearance and strategic patience: Imam Ali was initially passed over to lead the *ummah* after the death of the prophet Muhammad, but eventually was chosen to be the fourth caliph. Following the Arab conquest of Iran, the Persian influence in the Islamic empire eventually asserted itself with the rise of the Abbasid dynasty more than a century later. And time and again, Iranians succeeded in effectively co-opting their conquerors (Macedonians, Arabs, and Mongols) who needed their administrative skills to govern conquered territories; yet Iran preserved its distinct identity and survived all these trials.[118]

Paradoxically, despite this preference for the long game, Iranian behavior is often characterized by slap-dash improvisation and the pursuit of short-term gain at the expense of long-term advantage. Thus, while the leaders of the IRI are sometimes able tacticians, they are often poor strategists. This is best demonstrated by the tendency of Iranian politicians to overreach and to overplay their hand (see below). It remains to be seen whether this tendency will complicate efforts to implement the nuclear deal with Iran, which will require patience and restraint on Iran's part if it is to reap fully the benefits of the agreement.

Reciprocity, Proportionality, and the Use of Violence. Iran frequently takes a tit-for-tat approach to relations with other countries, responding in kind to actions by its adversaries, at a level broadly commensurate to the perceived challenge. This principle guides its response to threats, pressure, and the use of force. Thus:

- During the Iran-Iraq War, Iran answered attacks on its oil industry with attacks on shipping in the Gulf, announcing that if it could not export oil, no other country would be permitted to do so.[119] It responded to air raids on Tehran with rocket and missiles strikes on Iraqi cities, including Baghdad. And it threatened to respond to Iraqi chemical warfare with chemical attacks of its own.[120]

- In response to the dispatch of Israeli warships in 2009 through the Suez Canal to the Persian Gulf region, Iran sent warships through the Suez Canal to the Eastern Mediterranean.[121]

- In response to US demands that Iran not produce nuclear weapons, Iran demanded in 2010 that the US give up its nuclear arms.[122]

- When the UN passed Security Council Resolution 1929 (2010) authorizing member states to inspect Iranian shipping for cargo proscribed by UN resolutions, Iran insisted that it would do likewise to ships of countries involved in such searches.[123]

- In response to cyberattacks on its nuclear program discovered in 2010, sanctions on its financial and oil sectors in 2011-2012, and the assassination of Iranian nuclear scientists (in some cases using sticky bombs) between 2010-2012, Iran undertook a series of cyberattacks on US financial institutions and Saudi and Qatari oil companies in 2011-2012, and a series of attacks on Israeli diplomats in Georgia, India, and Thailand in February 2012 (some of which also used sticky bombs).[124]

Ayatollah Khamenei gave explicit voice to this longstanding principle in two recent speeches: an October 2011 speech at the Imam Ali Military Academy, in which he announced that Iran would answer "threats with threats," and his Nowruz 2012 speech (his major annual address), when he declared that "against an attack by enemies . . . we will attack them on the same level that they attack us."[125]

This insistence on reciprocity is rooted in the Islamic Republic's identity and worldview: the Shi'ite commitment to fighting "injustice," a determination to avoid a repetition of Iran's past national humiliations at the hands of Great Powers, and the rejection of perceived double standards (except when they benefit Iran) rooted in a "third-worldist" strand in the regime's ideology.[126] As Iran's leadership sees it, to agree to anything less would be to signal acceptance of second-class status unbefitting a revolutionary regime that sees itself as the guardian of Muslim honor and the modern embodiment of one of the world's great empires. Moreover, this approach builds legitimacy for Tehran's policies, since the Islamic Republic can say that it is only claiming what others claim for themselves, and demanding what is demanded of it.

Calculated Violence. The IRI generally uses violence in a calculated manner, often to achieve moral-psychological effects vis-à-vis its enemies.[127] For instance, the IRI took a measured approach toward the domestic opposition movement that arose in the wake of the contested June 2009 elections, building on lessons-learned from previous confrontations. It sought to prevail by wearing down and demoralizing the opposition over time, rather than by resorting to the massive use of force. There were no "Tiananmen Square moments" in the regime's efforts to quash the Green movement, nor did it play by "Hama rules."[128]

By providing security forces with sticks, batons, chains, and tear gas, and by generally avoiding live fire—in order to keep fatalities down—the regime precluded the mass public mourning ceremonies that energized the revolution against the Shah.[129] By ensuring that street clashes were bloody, close-quarter melees, it frightened off the less stout-hearted among the opponents of the regime.[130] And by mistreating, torturing, and humiliating detainees, and then releasing them so that they can tell their stories to their families and friends, it demoralized and intimidated the public.[131]

The IRI reserves the special institution of "house arrest"—which entails stigmatization, isolation, and marginalization—for its most dangerous domestic opponents. It used this technique for Ayatollah Khomeini's deposed heir, Ayatollah Hussein Ali Montazeri, and it has kept Green Movement leaders Mir Hussein Mousavi and Mehdi Karroubi under house arrest. House arrest is often tantamount to a life sentence that ends only with the death of the victim. It permits the regime to effectively "disappear" prominent individuals, while avoiding more drastic measures (such as imprisonment or extrajudicial killings) that could prompt a popular backlash or engender dissent within the regime's inner circle.[132]

The IRI has nevertheless sometimes acted against its enemies with abandon. Iran executed thousands of imprisoned oppositionists in 1988 during the final phases of the Iran-Iraq War (estimates range from 5,000-30,000). It likewise assassinated dozens of Iranian oppositionists living in Europe and elsewhere during the 1980s and early 1990s until the 1992 murder of Iranian Kurdish oppositionists in a Berlin restaurant caused a rupture in Iran's relations with Europe, by and large putting an end to this practice.

The Islamic Republic has struggled since the early days of the revolution to ensure its monopoly over the use of force. In part, this is because it has a history of radical elements taking action to force the hand of the government, and of the latter rewarding them afterwards if the gambit redounds to its benefit.[133] Thus, radical "students" occupied the US embassy in Tehran on November 4, 1979 to undermine efforts by the provisional government to reestablish normal ties with the US. (Khomeini did not know of the planned takeover beforehand, but provided his blessing after the fact.) Many of the young hostage takers went on to become prominent politicians and officials in the IRI.[134] The British embassy in Tehran was similarly occupied and ransacked in November 2011, with no adverse consequences for those involved.

Likewise, the commander of the IRGC Navy unit that detained 15 Royal Navy sailors and marines without authorization in the Shatt al-Arab in March 2007, was lauded and decorated when the episode ended well for the IRI, with the humbling of the UK.[135] While such "rogue" actions are infrequent, they have sometimes had dramatic consequences for Tehran's domestic politics and foreign relations.

The Moral, Spiritual, and Psychological. The IRI emphasizes the primacy of the moral, spiritual, and psychological dimensions of war over the physical and technological. According to Supreme Leader Khamenei's representative to the IRGC, Hojjat al-Eslam Ali Saidi,

> Our war with the dominant system [the US] is an asymmetrical war. What makes [it an even struggle] is the element of spirituality, motivation, and will. Spirituality is an effective element that

alters the equations of the combat field. Experience has proven that by using the element of spirituality and will, the most powerful enemy capability can be defeated.[136]

Tehran's approach to diplomacy and strategy thus often emphasizes achieving psychological effects over physical effects, and for this reason it often sees the informational line of operation as the decisive one in conflicts with adversaries. Whereas the United States undertakes information activities to support its military operations (hence the current name for psychological operations—Military Information Support Operations), Iran frequently undertakes military activities—exercises, shows of force, and proxy operations—to support its information operations.[137]

This approach draws, at least in part, on Islamic religious traditions, and the IRI's historical experience.[138] Thus, the Quran says, in Surat al-Anfal, verse 60: "Against them make ready your strength to the utmost of your power, including steeds of war, to strike terror into the hearts of the enemies of God, and your enemies." This verse, which appears in the official logo of the IRGC, underscores the importance of the psychological dimension of warfare. Likewise, Surat al-Anfal, verse 65 declares: "O Prophet! Rouse the believers, to the fight. If there are twenty amongst you, patient and persevering, they will vanquish two hundred; if a hundred, they will vanquish a thousand of the unbelievers." These verses essentially assert that success in war is a function of faith, and that religious zeal can compensate for lack of numbers.

The IRI's historical experience supports this approach. In the Shah's Iran, clandestinely distributed tape recordings of Ayatollah Ruhollah Khomeini's sermons contributed to the success of the Islamic Revolution and the rise of Khomeini as its leader, while skillful propaganda spurred mass defections from the Shah's armed forces and discouraged many still loyal to the old order. And during Hizballah's protracted guerrilla war against Israel in southern Lebanon (1982–2000), psychological operations played a central role in undermining Israeli domestic support for the occupation of southern Lebanon, contributing to its withdrawal in May 2000.

This mindset informs the regime's approach to both the domestic opposition and its external enemies. *Newsweek* correspondent Maziar Bahari offered unique insight into this belief system in an article about his detention by Iranian authorities in the wake of the June 2009 presidential election:

> I once interviewed a former Islamic guerrilla who had become a government minister. The problem with the shah's secret police, he said, was that they thought they could break a prisoner's will through physical pressure, but that often just hardened the victim's resolve. 'What our brothers after the revolution have masterminded is how to break a man's soul without using much violence against his body.'[139]

The amount of effort Tehran invests in information activities and its all-consuming preoccupation with alleged US efforts to foment a "soft revolution" through propaganda and psychological warfare (a reflection of the culture's conspiratorial worldview)[140] provide the most compelling proof of the importance the IRI attaches to the psychological dimension of statecraft and strategy. Indeed, IRGC commander-in-chief Mohammad Jafari stated on several occasions that the 2009 "sedition" against the Islamic Republic (i.e., the popular protests spearheaded by the Green Movement following that year's presidential elections) "was much more dangerous than the (eight-year) imposed war" with Iraq.[141] Likewise, the subordination of state-controlled radio and television to the IRI's intelligence and security services, demonstrates the importance assigned by the regime to information activities that could undermine the moral and spiritual well-being of the population.[142]

The reason for this preoccupation is not difficult to discern. Iran enjoys significant geographic depth, and the country's heavily populated central plateau is surrounded by a ring of rugged mountain ranges, which are a powerful deterrent to invasion. By contrast, each and every citizen is susceptible to subversive messages that enter the country through the internet, radio, and satellite television, and that have the potential to undermine support for the regime's revolutionary ideology.

This vulnerability is compounded by the fact that so many Iranians are attracted to Western popular culture.[143] As Supreme Leader Ali Khamenei said in a 2003 address on state television, "Iran's enemies" do not need "artillery, guns, and so forth" as much as they need "to spread cultural values that lead to moral corruption." He continued:

> They have said this many times. I recently read in the news that a senior official in an important American political center said: 'Instead of bombs, send them miniskirts.' He is right. If they arouse sexual desires in any given country, if they spread unrestrained mixing of men and women, if they lead youth to behavior to which they are naturally inclined by instincts, there will no longer be any need for artillery and guns against that nation.[144]

Accordingly, Iran has tried to create strategic depth in the informational domain by jamming foreign radio and TV broadcasts into Iran, banning social media, creating firewalls that make it difficult for average Iranians to access the world wide web, and working to create a stand-alone "national internet" to insulate its population from subversive foreign influences. These efforts have made it harder for Iranians to connect with the outside world, but have not cut them off from it.[145]

And to guard itself against subversive foreign cultural influences and enemy psychological warfare, the IRI has repeatedly tried to "Islamicize" the universities and the security forces and military, and to nurture a culture of resistance, jihad, and martyrdom in Iranian society, to foster their own kind of Islamic "societal resilience."

Resistance, Jihad, and Martyrdom. The IRI's efforts to cultivate a culture of resistance, jihad, and martyrdom built on the moral and spiritual values of the Islamic Revolution, are not only central to its efforts to insulate the Islamic Revolution against subversive foreign cultural influences, but are central to Iran's efforts to project influence and confront its enemies.

The concept of *moqavamat* (resistance) was adopted as a slogan by the Palestinian national movement in the 1960s, fashioned into a quasi-religious doctrine of armed struggle by the Palestinian Hamas and the Lebanese Hizballah in the 1980s, and subsequently appropriated by Iran and Syria. While the doctrine of resistance has foreign origins, it resonates with those who embrace the Shi'ite martyrdom narrative of Imam Hussein, who chose resistance and martyrdom at Karbala, over surrender to the forces of the unjust 7[h] century Caliph Yazid.

The "resistance doctrine" exhorts its adherents to stand fast in the face of enemy threats, to push boundaries, and eschew compromise on matters of principle in the belief that in a zero-sum struggle, compromise is a sign of weakness that will be exploited by the enemies of Islam.[146] It posits that victory is achieved by imposing costs and by demoralizing the enemy—through relentless psychological warfare, through terrorizing and bleeding its people and military, and by denying it battlefield victories.[147] The doctrine's claimed past successes in Lebanon and Gaza have emboldened Tehran to pursue a more assertive regional policy, and to undertake a policy of "nuclear resistance"—escalating tensions with many of its neighbors, the United States, and much of the international community.[148]

The IRI's efforts to promote a culture of resistance, jihad, and martyrdom also aims to create a society that is energized and strengthened by conflict.[149] Just as the death of protestors during the 1978-79 Islamic Revolution led to ever larger demonstrations—contributing to the success of the revolution—the IRI strives to create a society whose readiness to sacrifice is strengthened by conflict and martyrdom.[150] These efforts, however, have fallen short of this goal; Iran remains a society traumatized by the Iran-Iraq War, repeated bloody purges, and recurrent cycles of repression. The jihadi martyrdom culture is embraced mainly by hard-core Hizballahis and Basijis, who make up only a small, albeit influential, part of Iranian society.[151]

The operational imperatives that flow from the "resistance doctrine"—to stand fast, push boundaries, and eschew compromise—coexist uneasily, at best, with the pragmatism and flexibility embodied in the principle of the "expediency of the regime." This tension between the pragmatic needs of governance and statecraft, and the absolute imperatives of the regime's political and religious doctrines, has been a defining feature of Iranian decision making since the IRI's inception.[152]

Since the late-1980s, the approach embodied by the principle of expediency has prevailed, though perceived successes of the resistance doctrine in Lebanon (2000), Gaza (2005), Iraq (2003-present), and Syria (2011-present), and in nuclear negotiations with the P5+1/EU, could strengthen advocates of this approach in the foreign policy arena.

Complicating this picture further is the upsurge of mahdist (messianic) devotion in Iran, dating to the late 1990s, when conservative clerics quietly promoted the cult of the Mahdi in response to the emergence of the reform movement. Then President Mahmud Ahmadinejad politicized the cult of the Mahdi in order to advance his own political agenda, though he eventually abandoned his apocalyptic rhetoric when it became clear that it was hurting him politically. It is difficult to judge the depth and breadth of support for the mahdist current in Iranian society and its broader political implications, although, as best can be determined, violent apocalyptic sects are a miniscule, fringe phenomenon in today's Iran. Ever since Ahmadinejad's first term as president, political mahdism has remained a marginal phenomenon that has not influenced Iranian policy.[153]

In sum, the prominence of the resistance narrative raises the possibility that under certain circumstances, Iranian decision makers might follow a path that could inadvertently lead to a conflict with the United States, or that they might even welcome a limited conflict in order to rekindle the spirit of the Islamic revolution or achieve some other policy objective. Indeed, the resistance doctrine has already propelled Hizballah and Hamas into four destructive wars with Israel. The future trajectory of Iranian policy and the ultimate implications of Iran's emergence as a "nuclear power" will therefore likely depend on the relative strength of the contending orientations of expediency and resistance among key decision makers, and perhaps, to some extent, the degree to which they are influenced by messianic undercurrents that may be present in Iranian society.

Tactical Flexibility. Tehran will sometimes stand fast in the face of pressure or threats, while at other times it will back off when firmly challenged, seeking other pressure points or vulnerabilities to exploit. And it has a decidedly mixed record of following through on its own threats; it will deescalate when its interests require it to do so, often renewing the challenge at another time or place, under more favorable circumstances. Thus:

- Iran reneged on a 2010 decision to send a naval aid flotilla to Gaza (in an attempt to emulate a prior Turkish flotilla), when Israel reportedly warned the United Nations that it would act against it;[154]

- Iran backed off from threats to close the Strait of Hormuz in January 2012 following the imposition of new US and EU sanctions, when warned by the US that this would cross a red line;[155]

- After warning the United States in January 2012 that it should not return an aircraft carrier to the Persian Gulf, Iran backed down when Washington did so three weeks later.[156] However, it subsequently tried to shoot down an American UAV in the Persian Gulf in November of that year and again in March 2013;[157]

- After senior advisor to the Supreme Leader Ali Akbar Velayati warned Israel in January 2013 that an attack on Syria would be treated as an attack on Iran, the latter did nothing when Israeli aircraft subsequently bombed convoys in Syria with arms for Hizballah;[158]

- An Iranian transport aircraft and naval convoy attempting to deliver arms to Houthi forces in Yemen in April 2015 turned back after Saudi aircraft bombed the runways of Sanaa Airport, and a US carrier strike group intercepted the convoy. Iran then sent a "humanitarian" convoy with media aboard to score propaganda points.[159]

Iran has followed a similar pattern with regard to its nuclear and missile programs.

- After Iran's covert enrichment plant at Natanz was discovered in 2002, it attempted to build a smaller, less conspicuous one in a mountain at Fordow, whose existence was revealed in 2009.

- In response to the 2003 US invasion of Iraq, Iran apparently halted its "structured" weaponization program, likely to avoid giving the United States a justification for invading Iran, though it is believed to have continued with relatively inconspicuous weapons R&D work.[160]

- While implementing a voluntary enrichment freeze at Natanz from 2003-2005 in response to pressure from the EU3, Iran worked to resolve technical problems with its enrichment program, while continuing work on its conversion facility at Esfahan.[161]

- When Israeli Prime Minister Benjamin Netanyahu warned in his September 2012 speech to the UN General Assembly that the accumulation by Iran of more than 250kg of 20 percent enriched uranium would cross an Israeli red line, the latter ceased such activities.[162]

- And in response to criticism of its missile program—particularly alleged plans to build an intercontinental ballistic missile (ICBM)—Iran announced that it would not build missiles with a range of more than 2,000km, in an apparent attempt to allay European and American concerns.[163] Yet Iran continued work on its Satellite Launch Vehicle program, which could provide the technological foundation for an ICBM program in the future.[164]

Thus, while it has sometimes seemed like Iran was charging forward with its missile and nuclear programs—testing amid great fanfare the 2,000km+ range *Sejjil* solid fuel missile in 2008 and 2009 (there have been no tests since), announcing the planned construction of ten underground enrichment facilities in August 2010 (work apparently never went beyond site surveys for five of these sites), and more than doubling installed IR-1 centrifuges between late 2011 and late 2013, perhaps as a means of exerting counter-pressure on the P5+1 (adding 10,000 during this period for a total of more than 18,000 IR-1s)—it has also at times quietly stepped back to avoid crises, while continuing progress in other areas, or by other means. [165]

The tactical flexibility that characterizes much of Iranian policy is facilitated by the fact that Iranian officials often do not appear to be bound by past claims, threats, or commitments, or feel a need to reconcile inconsistencies. Statements are often issued in response to the needs of the moment (to impress an audience, create an effect, or save face) and are frequently forgotten as soon as they are uttered, if it is convenient to do so.[166] This may be rooted in an oft-noted tendency of Iranians to engage in dissimulation in routine daily interactions with family, friends, and professional colleagues, perhaps to smooth social relations in an agonistic society, or as a defense mechanism vis-à-vis autocratic governments and hostile foreign powers.[167]

This cavalier approach to language makes it difficult to know how seriously to take Iranian public pronouncements (or, for that matter, how to distinguish between ideological posturing and the articulation of deeply-held beliefs). Thus, in September 2012, at the height of concerns about a possible Israeli preventive strike against Iran's nuclear program, commander of IRGC aerospace forces Brig Gen Hajizadeh stated that if either Israel or the United States starts a war with Iran,

> it will be joined by the other one. We see the US and the Zionist regime standing fully on the side of each other and we cannot imagine the Zionist regime initiating a war without the US backup. Due to the same reason, if a war breaks out, we will definitely wage battle on both sides and will definitely be engaged with the US bases. In case such conditions arise, a series of incidents will take place which will not be controllable and manageable and such a war might turn into a third world war. That means, certain countries may enter the war for or against Iran.[168]

Yet, during this period, Iran was careful to use lethal force only against Israel in retaliation for unattributed attacks (such as the assassination of Iranian nuclear scientists). This raises the question whether threats to take on both the United States and Israel were more a bluff to bolster deterrence or to drive a wedge between Israel and the United States, rather than a preview of how the IRI would respond in such a scenario. At any rate, the IRI's track record makes it difficult to know when to take Iranian threats and warnings seriously, though experience would seem to indicate that the more they threaten publicly, the less likely they are to act—and vice versa.

Propensity to Overreach. The IRI has repeatedly demonstrated a tendency to be too clever by half or to overreach and to overplay its hand in its diplomacy, business dealings, and military activities. For instance, Tehran's:

- Unnecessary prolongation of the negotiations with the United States over the freeing of the embassy hostages contributed to the deep distrust that characterizes relations between the two countries to this day;

- Tendency to drag out negotiations "to the 61^s minute" in the pursuit of minor advantage, has often resulted in far less favorable outcomes for Iran than if it had taken a more flexible approach from the outset, and cost it many business opportunities;

- Decision to continue the Iran-Iraq War after 1982, when it could have had a cease-fire with Iraq, unnecessarily prolonged the war, leading to six more years of fighting that exacted a very high price in blood and treasure from Iran;

- Temporary occupation in December 2009 of a disputed oil well on the border with Iraq, embarrassed its allies in the Iraqi government and unnecessarily antagonized Iraqis of all persuasions;

- Intervention in Syria since 2011 has helped polarize the Middle East along sectarian lines, and contributed to an unprecedented jihadist mobilization on behalf of Syria. While this enabled Iran to rally to its side the 20 percent of the Middle East that is Shi'ite, it also convinced the 75 percent that is Sunni that Iran is a grave threat to their identity and interests, and brought together previously irreconcilable states—Turkey, Saudi Arabia, Qatar—in a Sunni axis against it;

- Pro-Houthi propaganda convinced the Saudis that Iranian support for the Houthis was a threat to their identity and their vital interests, causing Riyadh to organize an Arab coalition in March 2015 to intervene in the war in Yemen.

Among the reasons that Iranian officials often find it difficult to close a deal or end a dispute is a zero sum approach to conflicts which precludes compromise, and the fear that in a political system characterized by extreme factionalism, rivals will claim that they could have done better. Thus, the decision to end the Iran-Iraq War in 1988 and to temporarily suspend the enrichment of uranium in 2003 remain contentious issues in Iranian politics. Protestations by friendly Foreign Ministry officials to the contrary, there is often little sense of the utility of achieving mutually beneficial ("win-win") compromises or of striking deals. The emphasis is on getting all one can, and of avoiding concessions.

Experience from past nuclear negotiations between the EU3 (France, Germany and the United Kingdom) and Iran (2003-2005) shows that whereas Western diplomats often used constructive ambiguity to bridge gaps, Iranian diplomats exploited ambiguity to achieve unilateral advantage, taking a strictly legalistic approach regarding matters not clearly proscribed. Thus, when the Iranian side did not want to be specific about a certain point, it was a sure sign that the point needs to be clarified, to prevent Iran from later taking advantage of gaps or ambiguities. Moreover, Tehran would often cheat small to test limits, with the nature of the EU3 response shaping the nature of subsequent violations; Iran would then adapt its response in accordance with its assessment of what the EU3 had discovered, and how they had reacted.[169]

A good example of the often self-defeating tendency by Tehran to overplay its hand has been manifest in the negotiations between Russia and Iran regarding the sale of the S-300 surface-to-air missile, which have been ongoing for a decade and a half. According to a Russian military officer involved in past negotiations, in 1999 Iran approached Russia to buy the S-300.

> Russia agreed and asked for about $800 million, but Iran's military leaders were not happy with this figure and for several more years they tried to cut it down. Naturally, this did not suit Moscow. The haggling lasted until 2007, when finally Iran backtracked and agreed to accept Russia's original offer, a contract worth $800 million. The deal was made, but by that time it was too late.[170]

The deal was cancelled before it could be implemented, due to public revelation of a covert Iranian nuclear facility at Fordow in September 2009, and the passing in June 2010 of a UN ban on weapons transfers to Iran (UNSCR 1929), which Russia agreed to extend to the S-300. When negotiations over the S-300 were renewed in 2015, this dynamic apparently repeated itself—despite Iran's presumed keen interest in acquiring the S-300 or a suitable replacement—creating complications in the negotiations. According to a source close to the Russian Ministry of Defense,

> They say the Iranians are trying to squeeze juice out of us ... [They are] trying to get technology access, technology transfer, a good price, good terms of delivery, and they are pressing us by pointing out that we already cheated on them twice. They are also trying to leverage us by saying we need them as a market for civilian technologies such as the Sukhoi Superjet-100 and Tupolev Tu-204 passenger planes, so they are trying to get as much out of us as they can.[171]

The propensity to overreach could conceivably be very problematic during a crisis. Thus far, Iran has often been spared the military consequences of its tendency to overreach due to the forbearance of its enemies. US military restraint has been a major form of escalation control in the US-Iran relationship. But US restraint may have contributed to Tehran's decision in March 2011 to plot an attack on the Saudi ambassador in the United States, in the belief that it could do so with relative impunity. Should Iran again attempt to hit foreign interests on American soil or succeed in striking at US interests overseas, the United States might finally feel compelled to respond militarily, raising the possibility of war by miscalculation.[172]

The United States has tried to address this potential for miscalculation—especially in the Persian Gulf, where warships from both countries frequently operate in proximity to each other—by proposing confidence- and security-building measures (CSBMs) that could reduce the potential for unintended conflict. Iran has repeatedly rejected these. Thus, when then Chairman of the Joint Chiefs Adm. Michael Mullen broached the idea of a hotline between US and Iranian military commanders in the Gulf in September 2011, his suggestion was roundly rebuffed by the head of the IRGC Navy.[173] For Tehran, uncertainty enhances its leverage and strengthens its case for the departure of US forces from the Gulf, while CSBMs would only confirm an unpalatable status quo, whereby US warships patrol right off its coast. Accordingly, the potential for miscalculation remains.

Disaggregating Enemy Coalitions. The IRI has long tried to drive wedges in hostile coalitions. During the Iran-Iraq War, Iran conducted terror attacks against a number of Gulf Arab states and France and against neutral shipping in the Gulf, in order to compel these countries and the international community to cease their support for the Iraqi war effort. During nuclear negotiations with the EU3, Iran tried to play off the European countries against one another, and in more recent nuclear negotiations, it has frequently attempted to separate the United States from Europe, and Russia and China from the rest of the P5+1 by dangling before them the prospect of lucrative oil and gas contracts. And as previously mentioned, in response to attacks on its nuclear scientists (between 2010-2012) that were widely attributed to Israel, Tehran stated that it would hold both Israel and the US responsible for these actions, perhaps causing the US to pressure Israel to halt them.[174]

Michael Eisenstadt

NARRATIVES OF VICTORY: ALI, HASSAN, AND HUSSEIN

The IRI looks to Islamic history for exemplars and inspiration, and the first three Shi'ite Imams, Ali, Hassan, and Hussein, through their life-example, provide the three templates for victory embraced by the Islamic Republic.[175]

Ali (cousin and son-in-law of the prophet Muhammad, early convert to Islam, and renowned fighter who participated in nearly all the early battles of Islam) represents the heroic warrior who prevails by defeating his enemies in combat and imposing his will on them—the *Alavi* model.[176] This concept of victory is similar to the dominant conception of military victory held in the West.

Hassan (grandson of the prophet and Ali's oldest son) signed a treaty with the Caliph Muawiya in 661 C.E. following the death of Ali, in which he ceded his claim to the caliphate in the interest of avoiding a violent succession struggle and the shedding of blood among Muslims. Hassan's pragmatism is the basis of the doctrine of "heroic flexibility" which Supreme Leader Khamenei adduced as a justification for Iran's nuclear negotiations with the P5+1.[177]

Finally, Hussein (Hassan's younger brother) embodies the virtue of victory through resistance and martyrdom—the *Ashura'i* model. Hussein and his family and followers were massacred by the forces of the Caliph Yazid near Karbala on Ashura (the 10 h day of Muharram) in 680 C.E. for insisting that the caliphate pass on to the prophet's family. Through martyrdom, Hussein achieved a moral victory by fighting and dying for what is just.[178]

In certain circumstances, a military defeat may advance the objectives of the *ummah* more effectively than a victory. Thus, the martyrdom of Hussein at Karbala has inspired generations of Shi'ites. This line of thinking was reflected by former Army Chief of Staff Maj. Gen. Ali Shahbazi, who once stated that

> it is possible that the United States or some country instigated by it might start a military conflict…but it will not be able to end it.. because only Muslims believe that 'whether we kill or are killed, we are victorious.' Others do not think this way.[179]

In reality, while the IRI's leadership renders lip service to the ideal of martyrdom, its behavior demonstrates that it is very much focused on worldly success—on diplomatic and military victories. Thus, while martyrdom may be a highly lauded personal choice, the IRI's leadership will accommodate itself to unpalatable realities (if only temporarily) to avoid collective martyrdom. After all, the survival of the Islamic Republic is the regime's supreme value, and when martyrs are required for the cause, they can be recruited from among the IRI's Arab, Afghan, or Pakistani proxies and allies. Since the end of the Iran-Iraq War, losing men in combat is something that Tehran has tried to avoid at all cost. But it has become increasingly unavoidable, as the wars in Syria and Iraq yield a growing crop of martyrs, mainly from among the ranks of Iran's regional allies and proxy forces, but also from among the ranks of the IRGC.[180]

IMPLICATIONS FOR A "NUCLEAR" IRAN?

The foregoing discussion of the IRI's strategic culture can provide insights into Iran's past nuclear activities and suggest possible future trajectories for its nuclear program.

The Islamic Republic's nuclear program is not a crash effort; it has been ongoing for nearly thirty years now, and the nuclear deal between Iran and P5+1/EU—if fully implemented—will place significant constraints on its nuclear activities for the next 10-15 years. The slow progress of its nuclear program was partly a product of human resource constraints and technological bottlenecks, as well as a desire to obscure its clandestine activities and avoid rousing its enemies to action.

As a result, Tehran's preferred way forward has been slow, incremental progress. If Iran eventually does get the bomb, it will likely be the result of a clandestine slow motion breakout, rather than a rapid dash in plain sight—though a crisis or war could force Iran down the latter path.

Tehran will likely adhere to the key provisions of the nuclear deal for at least as long as is necessary to obtain sanctions relief and to attract sufficient foreign investment to make the reimposition of sanctions politically and economically unpalatable for the P5+1/EU—and perhaps for much longer if the benefits of compliance meet or exceed Iran's expectations. At the same time, Tehran will seek to limit the effectiveness of the IAEA's monitoring to preserve the option of engaging in low-signature weapons R&D work and other proscribed activities, without incurring excessive risk of compromise.

Iran may be willing to live with a latent or 'recessed' deterrent for many years, perhaps even after major constraints on its program are lifted.[181] In the long run, however, it will be sorely tempted to get the bomb, whether by creating an indigenous clandestine parallel program or by acquiring fissile material from abroad. Iran's nuclear proliferation calculus will depend on several factors: factional alignments in Tehran; the regional threat environment; the degree to which its leadership believes that an attempted clandestine break-out (or "sneakout") would be detected (which will depend on the effectiveness of IAEA and foreign intelligence monitoring, and Tehran's ability to obstruct both), and; the perceived risks and costs of getting caught.

For Iran, an interval of 10-15 years until it can resume its nuclear march (assuming the agreement lasts that long) is not an exceedingly long wait in the context of a thirty year old program, and a 6,000 year old civilization. Iran will also move forward with its missile program, which is not effectively constrained by the deal, as demonstrated by its test of a new missile, the *Emad*, in October 2015.

That said, assessing Tehran's decision calculus is always a fraught undertaking. Iran has often acted in ways that appeared contrary to its interests, and has sometimes assumed what appeared to be unreasonable risks; its logic is not always easy for outsiders, or even many Iranians, to understand.

If Iran acquires the bomb, it might be content to continue its policy of nuclear ambiguity and keep its nascent nuclear arsenal a secret until a crisis, war, or pride eventually cause it to unveil its capabilities. If it were to declare or test its nuclear capability in peacetime, Iran would probably do so (at least initially) to achieve political-psychological objectives: to enhance the regime's soft power and the IRI's leverage in the ongoing strategic competition with its Arab enemies, the United States, and Israel.[182]

Close to home, Iran is likely to use the aura of power created by its nuclear capabilities to persuade the Gulf states that their relationship with the United States puts them in jeopardy, that the United States cannot be relied on to protect them, and that they should deny access, basing, and overflight rights to the US military, and make their peace with Tehran—on the latter's terms. In so doing, Tehran would achieve its long sought-after goal of eliminating US influence in the Gulf, thereby gaining a free hand to deal with its neighbors as it sees fit. If they fail to do so, Iran may ramp up support for proxies to engage in subversion and terror in the Gulf states.

Iran's nuclear hedging and its pursuit of regional dominance could cause one or more of the region's Sunni states to hedge as well, eventually leading to a nuclear arms race in the region. Indeed, there are early signs that the process may have already started.[183] The ultimate implications of this development will depend on whether any succeed in eventually getting "the bomb," and the degree to which salafi-jihadist movements such as IS remain a threat to the stability and survival of these states.

Further abroad, as part of its campaign against Israel, Iran has built up the military capabilities of Hizballah in Lebanon and Hamas in Gaza. In the wake of the 2014 Gaza war, Supreme Leader Khamenei announced that Iran would arm the West Bank too—though with Israel and Jordan controlling access to this territory, it lacks the ability to translate this aspiration into reality at this time.[184] Meanwhile, Iran will continue to work with Hizballah to establish a base of operation in the Syrian Golan for proxy operations against Israel.[185]

Tehran's goal is to enmesh Israel in a series of protracted, bloody, inconclusive, and demoralizing conflicts

Michael Eisenstadt

with Iranian proxies along its borders, with the implied threat of nuclear annihilation ("Israel should be wiped off the map...") casting a pall over the future of the Jewish state.[186] The hope is that this will lead to mass emigration by those who have other options, and terminal decline.[187] This does not preclude the possibility that some Iranian officials might see nuclear terrorism as a viable option against Israel, though the threat posed by Israel's arsenal of 100-200 nuclear weapons will undoubtedly weigh heavily on more prudent Iranian decision makers.[188]

In the next decade or two, Iran may eventually deploy ICBMs, first with conventional, then perhaps with nuclear, warheads. Iran will be able to hold the United States and Western Europe at risk, in much the same way that US and Western European forces can now hold Iran's vital assets at risk.

Given the proliferation of sectarian and religious struggles in the region, Tehran's involvement in a number of these conflicts, and Iran's tendency to overreach and engage in reckless behavior, one does not have to believe Iran's leadership is "irrational" to be concerned that a nuclear exchange could result from a miscalculation or inadvertent escalation as a result of a conventional conflict in the Gulf or the Levant. The problem is not so much irrationality (at least as popularly understood), but the degree to which leaders may be oblivious to or tolerant of risk; motivated by emotions, ambitions, or delusions; or inclined to misread their own or adversary capabilities. History is replete with examples of apparently rational but insular, blinkered, or otherwise driven leaders who made tragic mistakes that led to the death of millions.[189]

Several other factors add extra layers of complexity to the picture: Short missile flight times and the absence of crisis hotlines between Tehran and its adversaries might cause regional states to adopt nuclear postures that include launch-on-warning or pre-delegation of launch authority to military commanders. Such steps could increase the risks of accidental or unauthorized use of nuclear weapons.[190]

The creation by Iran of a composite force of conventional and nuclear-armed missiles would add a profoundly destabilizing element to the mix; in a crisis or war, Israel, for instance, might not be able to discern whether missiles launched at it by Iran are conventional or nuclear, confronting it with the dilemma of absorbing what might turn out to be a devastating nuclear first strike, or launching a pre-emptive nuclear counter-strike in response to what might turn out to be a conventional attack.[191] Under such circumstances, Israel's nuclear forces would likely be kept on hair-trigger alert. Reckless and incendiary rhetoric by Iranian military officials—including ritual calls for the destruction of Israel—will incline Israeli decision makers to see Iranian actions in the most negative possible light.[192]

Tehran has shown no interest in confidence- and security-building measures that could reduce the potential for misunderstandings or miscalculation, because it believes that uncertainty enhances its leverage, while stability helps consolidate an unfavorable status quo. Hopefully, this aspect of its policy will change in the future, and Tehran will eventually agree to implement confidence building measures with all countries in the region, to reduce the potential for miscalculation.

A variety of factors, then, are likely to complicate efforts to prevent an Iranian nuclear breakout, and to create a stable deterrent balance with a nuclear Iran. As demonstrated in the past decade and a half, the Middle East is a "black swan" prone region: Consider the events of 9/11, the complications flowing from the 2003 US invasion of Iraq, and the events of the Arab uprisings of 2011 and since.[193]

So what does all this say about the public debate about Iranian "rationality" and nuclear deterrence? Clearly, there is little evidence that Iran is led by a "messianic apocalyptic cult"[194] for whom mutual assured destruction is "not a constraint" but "an inducement."[195] The IRI's conduct over the past three decades simply does not support this interpretation. But neither should much credence be given to facile claims that because deterrence worked during the Cold War, there is no reason it should not work with Iran.[196]

Such claims are based on a superficial and selective reading of the IRI's strategic conduct. For, while Iran's leadership has shown that it is "rational" and generally risk averse, it is also occasionally prone to reckless behavior and to overreach—tendencies which its far-reaching ambitions tend to amplify. A country's leaders do not have to be irrational to take irresponsible risks, with potentially catastrophic consequences. And this pattern of conduct could greatly complicate efforts to create a stable deterrent balance with a nuclear Iran.[197]

CONCLUSIONS

The IRI's strategic culture has had a profound impact on its approach to statecraft, strategy, and war. The result is an unconventional adversary that requires unconventional approaches to strategy and policy. This is most clearly manifest in the structure of the IRI's armed forces, which are organized to conduct terror, subversion, and proxy operations, naval guerilla warfare, and strategic bombardment campaigns. This non-traditional force structure has served the IRI well, deterring attacks on its homeland and on its nuclear program, and enabling Iran to exploit opportunities to expand its influence in the region since the onset of the Arab uprisings in 2011.

But the IRI also has major vulnerabilities: lacking integrated air defenses, Iran's critical infrastructure is vulnerable to airstrikes; its terror apparatus is not as capable as it once was, and can no longer be relied on to strike at targets on several continents at will; its navy can deliver sharp blows, but would not survive sustained combat with a modern, diversified air-sea battle team; and its missile force may have trouble penetrating, in large numbers, defenses in Israel or the Gulf.

To preserve this comparative advantage, the US should work to prevent Iran from acquiring weapons that could round out its force structure and fill key capabilities gaps, mitigate critical vulnerabilities, and neutralize US advantages. Indeed, there are already indications that Iran is increasing its defense budget to ramp up procurement of missiles and conventional arms.[198] Thus, the United States should continue diplomatic efforts to prevent Iran from obtaining game-changing weapons such as the Russian S-300 SAM.[199] And it should continue to encourage its allies to acquire capabilities that can exploit Iranian vulnerabilities and counter Iranian strengths (such as long-range strike fighters and missile defenses, respectively).[200]

Countering Tehran's Deterrence/Warfighting Triad. To deter or defeat Tehran, the United States needs to counter each element of Iran's deterrent and warfighting triad so that the Islamic Republic will have little confidence in its ability to harm US interests, achieve its own objectives, or terminate a conflict on favorable terms. While the United States has made much progress in countering Iran's capabilities in all three areas, important gaps remain:

Terror, Subversion, and Proxy Warfare. The United States and Israel have succeeded in recent years in disrupting a number of Qods Force and Hezbollah activities and operations, due to significant improvements in counterterror capabilities, enhanced international counterterror cooperation since 9/11, and the atrophying of IRGC and Hezbollah capabilities in this area since the 1990s.[201]

On the other hand, the IRI has been successful at filling power vacuums created by the Arab uprisings and the rise of IS, by heavy reliance on proxy forces, limited use of Qods Force advisors, the judicious commitment of IRGC combat personnel, and the use of its diplomatic, informational, and economic levers. These interventions have transformed the geopolitics of the region, confounding claims that the IRI's regional influence is self-limiting.[202]

Iran's activities in this domain are best countered by a "whole-of-government" approach that likewise relies on proxies, limited force, and diplomatic, informational, and economic tools to roll back Iranian influence.[203] In this area, the United States is lagging.

Naval Guerilla Warfare. The United States has been playing catch-up in recent years in its efforts to counter Tehran's anti-access capabilities. While it is much better positioned today than it was a few years ago, it still has a way to go to counter the threat from naval mines, midget submarines armed with advanced torpedoes, small-boat swarms, suicide UAVs, highly capable anti-ship cruise missiles, and anti-ship

Michael Eisenstadt

ballistic missiles.[204]

Strategic Bombardment/Missile Warfare. The United States and its Israeli and Gulf allies have been investing significant resources in missile defense in recent decades (and, in the case of Israel, rocket defense as well). America and its Gulf partners, however, still face major challenges: insufficient numbers of interceptors to deal with Iranian saturation tactics, gaps in the coverage of currently deployed missile defenses, and the lack of an integrated missile defense architecture in the Gulf.[205]

Iran, moreover, has become increasingly reliant on cyber operations to push back against the United States and its allies, while Washington has been extremely cautious in responding to Iranian cyberattacks. It apparently lacks both the ability to protect its critical infrastructure against sophisticated attacks, as well as a strategy for dealing with them.[206] Yet, US cyber capabilities could contribute to nonproliferation if paranoia about foreign cyber spying leads Tehran to conclude that an attempted nuclear "sneakout" would quickly be detected.

Tailored Approaches and Capabilities. The foregoing assessment about the IRI's strategic culture also yields a number of conclusions pertaining to deterrence, soft warfare, and information activities, which might require major changes in how the US government thinks about, and is organized to accomplish each of these tasks vis-à-vis Iran.

Deterrence. Deterrence should be tailored to the IRI's value system and must take into account the 35 year history of the Islamic Republic and the United States; intuitive or cookie-cutter approaches that do not incorporate these factors are liable to fail.[207] To this end, the United States needs to, first of all, understand the IRI's red lines, so that it does not inadvertently cross them, thereby leading to an unintended conflict.

Conversely, because Tehran is occasionally prone to take risks and to overreach, the US must be absolutely clear about its own red lines; here, ambiguity is not constructive. Washington must also push back against efforts by Tehran to test or circumvent US red lines. Failure to do so will only invite additional challenges.

Yet, the US should be flexible in how it communicates threats. It should communicate these directly when necessary, and employ subtle, implied threats that play on Iranian paranoia when direct, overt threats might cause the IRI to dig in its heels to save face, or when overt threats are deemed inappropriate (for instance, during high profile diplomatic negotiations).

The US also needs to repair its credibility gap vis-à-vis Iran: for more than thirty years Washington has taught Tehran that it can wage proxy warfare against it without risking a military response or paying an unacceptable cost. (The sole exception that proves the rule is the series of naval engagements in the Persian Gulf during the US-led tanker escort operations toward the end of the Iran-Iraq War.)

To alter this dynamic, Washington must demonstrate through words and actions that it is increasingly tolerant of risk in its dealings with Tehran, and push back against Iranian policies that harm its interests. Otherwise, Tehran may continue pushing boundaries, increasing the risk of an unintended confrontation with the United States.

The US should further work to deny Tehran the ability to hold US interests and assets at risk by continuing to encourage alternative oil export routes that bypass the Strait of Hormuz,[208] and by reducing the exposure of forward deployed forces in the Gulf (such as Carrier Strike Groups) to highly capable Iranian anti-access systems during times of tension. For instance, this might entail the adoption of "outside-in" approaches to securing the Strait of Hormuz.[209]

And while missile defense and mine countermeasure exercises are necessary elements of an effective deterrence posture toward Iran, they are not sufficient; it is also necessary to conduct exercises that simulate long-range strike operations and the projection of power deep into the adversary's territory.

In interactions with Iran, the US should, therefore, emphasize both deterrence by denial and deterrence by punishment. US officials have tended, in recent years, to emphasize deterrence by denial in public statements directed at Iran, asserting that the US has sufficient capabilities to thwart Iranian objectives. But this permits Tehran to calibrate and manage risk, which may lower the threshold for action, and make miscalculation more likely.[210]

The US should also emphasize that it will hold vital Iranian assets at risk, and that it will not necessarily retaliate symmetrically in the event of a conflict. This will make the US a more unpredictable adversary, thereby raising the potential costs of miscalculation, and bolstering deterrence.

Last, but not least, US information activities should assure allies by highlighting America's ability to counter Iranian capabilities, while strengthening deterrence by underscoring the latter's vulnerability to retaliation (especially its oil industry, which is concentrated along its long and vulnerable coastline).

Soft Warfare. Because the IRI's leadership came to power through revolution, survival remains its foremost concern, and counterrevolution its greatest fear. It believes that US soft warfare—efforts to inculcate foreign ideas, values, and ideologies in order to undermine the Islamic Republic—is a greater threat to the regime's survival than a foreign military strike or invasion.

This is a fear that the United States should play on to pressure Tehran, and to bolster deterrence. To do so, the United States needs to revive its ability to wage political warfare—the use of all instruments of national power short of war—to advance its national interest. These might include inform and influence activities, sabotage and subversion campaigns, economic warfare, and covert action to destabilize the Islamic Republic.[211] The threat of soft/political warfare has the potential to be one of the most effective instruments in the US toolkit, vis-à-vis Iran.

This, however, is easier said than done. America's capabilities in this domain have atrophied since the Cold War. Skills have to be relearned and capabilities reestablished. And it is much easier to do harm than good through crude or maladroit influence activities, or amateurish or bungled covert operations.

Moreover, most of America's soft power resides in the private sector—its popular and consumer culture, Hollywood, its information technology sector, and its higher education system—and cannot be effectively mobilized by the US government to serve as an instrument of US foreign policy. Yet to the degree that the United States seeks to promote its values and advance its interests by expanding contacts between peoples, fostering the free exchange of ideas and information, and opening markets to American cultural and commercial products, it helps facilitate the flow of information and ideas to Iran.[212]

To this end, the United States should more actively encourage the private sector to build bridges with Iranian civil society. In many cases, private organizations already have missions that would serve US purposes: news outlets want to get information out; universities want to encourage contact, scholarly exchange, and debate; entertainment companies want to provide types of music and images that the Iranian people want but the regime hates. On this count, the US government is already encouraging the private sector to find ways to help Iranians circumvent limits on their ability to get news and to communicate with each other, but it needs to do more.[213]

Undoubtedly there will be objections to meddling in Iran's internal affairs, and to any actions resembling the Anglo-American coup in 1953 that removed Prime Minister Mohammad Mosaddeq. While such concerns are understandable, keeping such an option in reserve, to be used *in extremis*, in the event of a major crisis between the two countries, could enhance US leverage and bolster deterrence.

Information Activities. The use of words, actions, and evocative images as part of a sustained campaign to influence opinion and shape the psychological environment in Iran is the greatest untapped source of US leverage over the Islamic Republic.[214] Information activities are often the IRI's decisive line of operations, and it will frequently undertake diplomatic and military activities to achieve an informational or psychological effect. The US, however, considers such activities of secondary importance at best. It has therefore not reaped the benefits that aggressive information campaigns might yield.

Iran engages in incessant propaganda and spin to burnish its reputation at home and abroad, and to discredit the United States. Accordingly, the United States needs to work incessantly to counter the IRI's spin, challenge its narrative, discredit its "resistance" doctrine through the defeat of its proxies, and highlight the price that the Iranian people have paid for Iran's support for radical movements and the Asad regime in Syria. Finally, the US should exploit Tehran's tendency to overreach to make the regime look foolish and incompetent in the eyes of its people, and the peoples of the region.

Countering Iran's Long Game. Finally, Iran's strategies of indirection, delay, and attrition are predicated, at least in part, on the assumption that time works in its favor. Iran's own experience demonstrates the risks of inconclusive protracted struggles. Iran was compelled to end the Iran-Iraq War without anything to show for its massive investment of blood and treasure. As the war ground on, and Tehran proved unable to achieve a military decision, Iran's isolation, Arab financial and military support for Iraq, and the latter's ability to acquire large quantities of arms on the international market, tilted the military balance in Iraq's favor.

Iran once again faces substantial challenges that could derail its long game: popular discontent with the status quo, major economic challenges, and the uncertain long-term prospects of its bloodied Hizballah proxy and its now enfeebled Syrian client. The nuclear deal, which will lift the most onerous sanctions on Iran, will in the near-term provide it with a much needed financial boost and breather, though it is unclear whether in the mid-to-long term the deal will live up to the expectations of both sides, or remain in force for more than a few years. The most that can be said for now is that the deal has potentially redefined the nature and terms of Iran's relationship with the international community, while likely deferring resolution of the most important issues pertaining to its nuclear program and status—perhaps indefinitely. As for Iran, the only thing that can be said with some degree of confidence is that its long game and the ceaseless pursuit of advantage will continue.

A Final Word. The nuclear deal between Iran and the P5+1/EU has raised hopes for an eventual rapprochement with the Islamic Republic. That will depend, to some extent, on how the deal performs. If both Iran and the United States eventually conclude that their interests were served by the agreement and that the other side largely adhered to its commitments, the accord may be a harbinger of further limited cooperation, albeit within an overall policy context still defined by competition and conflict.

However, ominous signs abound. Tehran has declared that it will not be bound by the arms sales and missile testing restrictions contained in the UN resolution (UNSCR 2231) that backstops the nuclear deal. It has announced that IAEA inspectors will not be permitted to visit military sites, potentially creating sanctuaries where proscribed activities can occur. And there is good reason to believe that the deal may not yield Iran the economic benefits it had hoped for.[215]

Supreme Leader Khamenei has likewise banned further negotiations with the United States (though this might not preclude tacit cooperation if it is in Iran's interest to do so), and he continues to spout anti-American invective.[216] For this reason, truly meaningful change in Iran-US relations will likely have to await his passing from the scene. Even so, anti-Americanism will remain deeply rooted in the IRI's political culture, and will be difficult to expunge from the system. And as always, the IRI's bifurcated governmental structure, consisting of traditional state institutions and of parallel revolutionary organs (especially the IRGC) that attempt to keep them in check, will greatly complicate efforts to improve relations.[217]

For these reasons, despite the potential for discrete cooperation, Iran-US relations will likely remain tense and fraught in the coming years, while the factors shaping Tehran's strategic behavior will remain largely unchanged. With the IRI remaining a difficult policy challenge and its nuclear potential set to grow in the coming years (whether or not the nuclear agreement remains in force), understanding the logic guiding and the factors driving Iran's strategic conduct will be more important than ever before.

Notes:

Barak A Salmon and Paula Holmes-Eber, *Operational Culture for the Warfighter Principles and Applications* (Quantico, VA: Marine Corps University Press, 2008)

[2] For a fascinating sketch of how Iranians and Americans tend to differ in temperament and outlook, see Dr Nassir Ghaemi, "The Psychology of Iranian-American Relations," *Psychology Today*, February 2, 2009, http://www.psychologytoday.com/blog/mood-swings/200902/the-psychology-iranian-american-relations

[3] Dima Adamsky, *Soviet, Russian, and Israeli Assessments of Iran's Nuclear Strategic Culture*, Long Term Strategy Group, September 2009, 48

[4] Patrick Clawson and Michael Rubin, *Eternal Iran Continuity and Chaos* (New York: Palgrave MacMillan, 2005), 93-95, 15-16, 27-28, 16-62, and passim

Abbas William Sami, "The Iranian Nuclear Issue and Informal Networks," *Naval War College Review*, Vol 59, No (Winter 2006), 64-90, https://www.usnwc.edu/getattachment/e904628-0224-4587-ad8f-c4ce204b2cd/Iranian-Nuclear-Issue-and-Informal-Networks-The--aspx

[6] Strategic culture consists of "shared beliefs, assumptions, and modes of behavior, derived from common experience and accepted narratives that shape collective identity and relationships to other groups, and which determine appropriate ends and means for achieving security objectives" Jeannie L Johnson and Jeffrey A Larsen, Comparative Strategic Cultures Syllabus, prepared by SAIC for Defense Threat Reduction Agency Advanced Systems and Concepts Office, 20 November 2006, at: http://www.fas.org/irp/agency/dod/dtra/syllabus.pdf For a useful overview of the origins and evolution of this concept, see Jeffrey S Lantis and Darryl Howlett, "Strategic Culture" in John Baylis, James J Wirtz, Colin S Gray, and Eliot Cohen (Eds), *Strategy in the Contemporary World* (Oxford, UK: Oxford University Press, 2007), 82-100 For previous works on Iranian strategic culture, see: Jennifer Knepper, "Nuclear Weapons and Iranian Strategic Culture," *Comparative Strategy*, Vol 27, No 5, 2008, 451-468; Will Stanley, "Iranian Strategic Culture and its Persian Origins," in Jeannie L Johnson, Kerry M Kartchner, and Jeffrey A Larsen, *Strategic Culture and Weapons of Mass Destruction* (Palgrave Macmillan: 2009), 137-156; Kamran Taremi, "Iranian Strategic Culture: The Impact of Ayatollah Khomeini's Interpretation of Shiite Islam," *Contemporary Security Policy*, Vol 35, No , 2014, 3-25, and; J Matthew McInnis, *Iran's Strategic Thinking Origins and Evolution*, American Enterprise Institute, May 12, 2015, https://www.aei.org/publication/irans-strategic-thinking-origins-and-evolution/

[7] Shaul Bakhash, *The Reign of the Ayatollahs Iran and the Islamic Revolution* (New York: Basic Books, 1990), 273

[8] Gregory F Giles, "Deterring a Nuclear-Armed Iran from Adventurism and Nuclear Use," in *Tailored Deterrence Influencing States and Groups of Concern*, eds Barry Schneider and Patrick Ellis (Maxwell Air Force Base, AL: US Air Force Counterproliferation Center, May 20), -36

[9] Ervand Abrahamian, "The Paranoid Style in Iranian Politics," in *Khomeinism Essays on the Islamic Republic* (Los Angeles: University of California Press, 1992), -3 ; Ahmed Ashraf, "Conspiracy Theories," *Encyclopedia Iranica*, December 15, 1992, http://iranica.com/articles/conspiracy-theories

[10] A possible exception to this trend was the bombing by a Hizballah operative of an Israeli-operated tour bus in Burgas, Bulgaria in July 2012

Martin Kramer, "Sacrifice and 'Self-Martyrdom' in Shi'ite Lebanon," in Martin Kramer (ed), *Arab Awakening and Islamic Revival* (New Brunswick, NJ: Transaction Publishers, 1996), 231-243, http://www.martinkramer.org/sandbox/reader/archives/sacrifice-and-self-martyrdom-in-shiite-lebanon/ Regarding Iran's Shiite allies in Iraq, see Michael Eisenstadt, Michael Knights, and Ahmed Ali, *Iranian Influence in Iraq Countering Tehran's Whole-of-Government Approach*, The Washington Institute for Near East Policy, Policy Focus No , Apr 20 , http://www.washingtoninstitute.org/pubPDFs/PolicyFocus pdf

[12] Likewise, Iran has supported Christian Armenia in its struggle against Shiite-majority Azerbaijan And since the demise of the Soviet Union, Iran has acted with restraint in the Caucasus and Central Asia, eschewing efforts to export the revolution to the Soviet Union's former Muslim republics, instead working with Russia to ensure stability in the region In both cases, geopolitics has trumped ideology

Michael Eisenstadt

[3] Asghar Sch raz , *The Constitution of Iran Politics and the State in the Islamic Republic* (New York: I B Taurus, 997), 233-246

[4] Dav d Menashr , *Revolution at a Crossroads Iran's Domestic Politics and Regional Ambitions*, (Wash ngton, DC: The Wash ngton Inst tute for Near East Po cy, 997), 8

[5] Robert Pear, "Khome n Accepts 'Po son of End ng the War w th Iraq; U N Send ng M ss on," *New York Times*, Ju y 2 , 988 http://www nyt mes com/ 988/07/2 /us/khome n -accepts-po son -of-end ng-the-war-w th- raq-un-send ng-m ss on htm

[6] When ja ed Iran an act v st Abdo ah Momen asked h s nterrogators why they used bruta methods such as to ture to extract confess ors, they responded that "accord ng to the founder of the Is am c Repub c the preservat on of the reg me s the foremost ob gat on " Letter of Prom nent Pr soner of Consc ence, Abdo ah Momen , to Ayato ah Khamane , Internat ona Campa gn for Human R ghts n Iran, September 9 20 0, http://www ranhumanr ghts org/20 0/09/ etter-momen -khamane

[7] Wh e *maslahat* was an estab shed pr nc p e n Sunn jur sp udence, Khome n s nnovat on was to app y t n the po t ca doma n to dea w th the cha enges of modern governance and to ensure the surv va of the Is am c Repub c Thus, Khome n ru ed that n the event of an apparent conf ct between government and shar a, the needs of the former take precedence, as the surv va of the Is am c Repub c s the on y way to ensure the mp ementat on of shar a and the surv va of ts brand of revo ut onary Is am Mehd Kha aj , persona correspondence, September 27, 20 5

[8] "Defence M n ster Comments on Product on of Shahab-3 M ss e," V s on of the Is am c Repub c of Iran Network 2, Tehran, Ju y 30, 998, trans ated n BBC Mon tor ng Summary of Wor d Broadcasts, August 3, 998

[9] Shahram Chub n, "Iran s 'R sk-Tak ng n Perspect ve," IFRI Secur ty Stud es Center, *Proliferation Papers*, No 2 , W nter 2008, https://www fr org/en/pub cat ons/enotes/pro ferat on-papers/ rans-r sk-tak ng-perspect ve

[20] Matthew Lev tt, *Hezbollah The Global Footprint of Lebanon's Party of God* (Wash ngton, DC: Georgetown Un vers ty Press, 20 3) 22-48 See a so D Peterson et a v The Is am c Repub c of Iran, M n stry of Fore gn Affa rs and the M n stry of Informat on and Secur ty, Un ted States D str ct Court, D str ct of Co umb a, Docket No CA 0 -2684, March 7, 2003

[2] Lev tt, *Hezbollah*, 75- 6; N cho as B anford, *Warriors of God Inside Hezbollah's Thirty-Year Struggle Against Israel* (New York: Random House, 20), 97, 98, 5; Dan e Byman, *A High Price The Tr umphs and Failures of Israeli Counterterrorism* (Oxford: Oxford Un vers ty Press, 20), 222-224

[22] Iran Human R ghts Documentat on Center, *Murder at Mykonos Anatomy of a Political Assassination*, March 2007, http://www rarhrdc org /eng sh/pub cat ons/reports/3 50-murder-at-mykonos-anatomy-of-a-po t ca -assass nat on htm

[23] Lev tt, *Hezbollah*, 8 -207; Lou s J Freeh, "Khobar Towers," *Wall Street Journal*, June 23, 2006 http://www wsj com/art c es /SB 5 0270256878833 ; USA v Ahmed a -Mughass et a , Ind ctment, US D str ct Court, Eastern D str ct of VA, A exandr a, VA, No 0 -228-A, June 200

[24] Dav d Cr st, *Gulf of Conflict A History of U.S.-Iranian Confrontation at Sea*, The Wash ngton Inst tute for Near East Po cy, Po cy Focus No 95, June 2009, 25-26, http://www wash ngton nst tute org/pubPDFs/Po cyFocus95 pdf

[2] Un ted States of Amer ca v Manssor Arbabs ar and Gho am Shakur , Ind ctment, Southern D str ct of New York, October , 20 , http://www just ce gov/s tes/defau t/f es/opa/ egacy/20 / 0/ /us-v-arbabs ar-shakur -comp a nt pdf

[26] "Attack on UK embassy n Iran 'had support of the state , *BBC News*, December 3, 20 , http://www bbc com/news/uk- 60 0547

[27] Neeraj Chauhan, "Cops Name Iran M tary Arm for Attack on Israe D p omat," *Times of India*, Ju y 30, 20 2, http://m t mesof nd a com /c ty/de h /Cops-name-Iran-m tary-arm-for-attack-on-Israe -d p omat/a t c eshow/ 52630 3 cms

[28] Iran has ong referred to the Iran-Iraq War as the " mposed war" because Iraq nvaded Iran But t may a so see t as the " mposed war" because

major convent ona war s not the IRI s preferred "way of war"

[29] Mehd Kha aj , "A Dea Among Enem es," *Caravan*, October 6, 20 5, http://www hoover org/research/dea -among-enem es

[30] Dav d Ignat us, "Ta k Bo d y W th Iran," *Washington Post*, June 23, 2006, http://www wash ngtonpost com/wp-dyn/content/art c e/2006/06/22 /AR200606220 469 htm

[3] "Sanaa s the fourth Arab cap ta to jo n the Iran an revo ut on," *Middle East Monitor Memo*, September 27, 20 4, https://www m dd eeastmon tor com/news/m dd e-east/ 4389-sanaa- s-the-fou th-arab-cap ta -to-jo n-the- ran an-revo ut on; A Younes ,"Adv sor To Iran an Pres dent Rohan : Iran Is An Emp re, Iraq Is Our Cap ta ," *MEMRI Dispatch* 599 , March 9, 20 5, http://www memr org/report /en/pr nt847 htm

[32] M chae Conne , "Iran s M tary Doctr ne," n Rob n Wr ght (ed), *The Iran Primer*, (Wash ngton, DC, Un ted States Inst tute of Peace: 20 0), http:// ranpr mer us p org/resource/ rans-m ta y-doctr ne

[33] Abbas Qa dar , "More p anes, more m ss es, more warsh ps: Iran ncreases ts m tary budget by a th rd," *Al-Monitor*, Ju y 3, 20 5, http://www a -mon tor com/pu se/or g na s/20 5/07/khamene -orders- ncrease-m tary htm

[34] It rema ns to be seen, however, whether the actua amount of sanct ons re ef and fore gn nvestment w   meet expectat ons Patr ck C awson, "W   the Obama Adm n strat on Imp ement the Str ngent Sanct ons Author zed Under the Iran Agreement?" The Wash ngton Inst tute for Near East Po cy, *PolicyWatch* 2476, August 2 , 20 5, http://www wash ngton nst tute org/po cy-ana ys s/v ew/w -the-obama-adm n strat on- mp ement -the-str ngent-sanct ons-author zed

[3] "Khamene : Iran W   Str ke Back f Attacked," *CBS News*, March 20, 20 2, http://www cbsnews com/830 -202_ 62-57400874/khamene - ran -w - str ke-back- f-attacked; Speech by Supreme Leader Ayato ah A Khamene at the Imam A M ta y Academy, October , 20 , http://eng sh khamene r/ ndex php?opt on com_content&task v ew& d 558&Item d 4

[36] "Deputy Top Commander: Crush ng Response Wa t ng for US M tary Threats Aga nst Iran," *Fars News Agency*, Ju y 3, 20 5, http://eng sh farsnews com/newstext aspx?nn 39404 2000454

[37] Marcus George and Zahra Hosse n an, "Iran W   Destroy Israe C t es f Attacked: Khamene ," *Reuters*, March 2 , 20 3, http://www reuters com /a t c e/20 3/03/2 /us- ran-khamene - dUSBRE92K0LA20 3032 ;"Iran an Top Commander: Z on sts Attack aga nst Iran Ends n Raz ng Israe ," *Fars News Agency*, Ju y 0, 20 5, http://eng sh farsnews com/newstext aspx?nn 39404 9000998

[38] "Commander: IRGC W   Destroy 35 US Bases n Reg on f Attacked," *Fars News Agency*, Ju y 4, 20 2, http://eng sh2 farsnews com /newstext php?nn 9 03084990

[39] "We We come No War, Nor do We In t ate Any War, But f Any War Happens, the One Who W   Emerge Loser W   be the Aggress ve and Cr m na U S ," Ayato ah A Khamene , tw tter feed of Ju y 25, 20 5, https://tw tter com/khamene _ r; "IRGC Off c a : US Boastfu Remarks about M tary Opt on aga nst Iran Source of Mockery," *Fars News Agency*, August 2, 20 5, http://eng sh farsnews co/newstext aspx?nn 394052 00 042

[40] M chae E senstadt and A on Paz, "Iran s Evo v ng Mar t me Presence," The Wash ngton Inst tute for Near East Po cy, *PolicyWatch* 2224, March 3, 20 4, http://www wash ngton nst tute org/po cy-ana ys s/v ew/ rans-evo v ng-mar t me-presence

[4] Even those Iran an off c a s work ng to ach eve a modus v vend w th Wash ngton tend to see the Un ted States as an mp acab e enemy and therefore a m to more effect ve y manage the re at onsh p, rather than transform t Thus, n May 20 3, wh e runn ng for Pres dent, Hassan Rouhan to d a group of Iran an expatr ates that "Today, we cannot say that we want to e m nate the tens on between us and the Un ted States… We shou d be aware that we can have nteract ons even w th the enemy n such a manner that the grade of ts enm ty wou d be decreased, and second y, ts enm ty wou d not be effect ve " Steven D tto, "Who s Hassan Rouhan ?" The Wash ngton Inst tute for Near East Po cy, *PolicyWatch* 2 47,

September 24, 20 3, http://www wash ngton nst tute org/po cy-ana ys s/v ew/who- s-hassan-rouhan

[42] Th s s a compos te sketch based on Iran an med a reports See, for nstance, the comments n Apr 20 3 by the po t ca deputy to the Supreme Leader s representat ve to the IRGC, Br g Gen Second C ass Yado ah Javan , n W Fu ton, Iran News Round Up, Apr 6, 20 3, http://www rantracker org/ ran-news-round-apr - 6-20 3; Pres dent Hassan Rouhan s comments n a speech to IRGC commanders n September 20 3 quoted n W Fu ton and Am r Toumaj, Iran News Round Up, September 6, 20 3, http://www rantracker org/ ran-news-round-september - 6-20 3; and IRGC Navy Commander RADM A Fadav s comments from a September 20 3 speech n W Fu ton and Am r Toumaj, Iran News Round Up, September 8, 20 3, http://www rantracker org/ ran-news-round-september- 8-20 3

[43] Conne , "Iran s M ta y Doctr ne"

[44] Thus, Iran an Ch ef of the Armed Forces Genera Staff Maj Gen Hassan F rouzabad stated n June 20 4 that "The Is am c Revo ut on has been expo ted to var ous cu tures and countr es… [The Un ted States] thought one day that war w th the Is am c Repub c of Iran cou d take p ace ke (s c) Iraq and Afghan stan However, they know today that a war w th [Iran] w engu f the g obe; therefore, they must destroy our power from w th n " Mehrdad Moaref an, Iran News Round Up, June 0, 20 4, http://www cr t ca threats org/ ran-news-round-June- 0-20 4

[4] Far bo z Haghshenass, "Iran s Doctr ne of Asymmetr c Nava Warfare," Wash ngton Inst tute for Near East Po cy, *PolicyWatch* 79, December 2 , 2006, at: http://www wash ngton nst tute org/temp ateC05 php?CID 2548; Far bo z Haghshenass, *Iran's Asymmetr c Nava Warfare*, Po cy Focus No 87, September 2008, http://www wash ngton nst tute org/pubPDFs/Po cyFocus87 pdf; M chae E senstadt *Iran an Military Power Capabilities and Intentions* (Wash ngton, DC: The Wash ngton Inst tute for Near East Po cy, 996), 48-62

[46] E senstadt and Paz, "Iran s Evo v ng Mar t me Presence"

[47] M chae E senstadt, "M ss es and the Nuc ear Negot at ons w th Iran," The Wash ngton Inst tute for Near East Po cy, *PolicyWatch* 2450, Ju y 6, 20 5, http://www wash ngton nst tute org/po cy-ana ys s/v ew/m ss es-and-the-nuc ear-negot at ons-w th- ran

[48] Warren R chey, "Iran ans Awa t Iraq Attacks n Campgrounds and Luxu y Hote s," *Christian Science Monitor*, Apr 5, 988,

[49] Ca t n Ta madge, "C os ng T me: Assess ng the Iran an Threat to the Stra t of Hormuz," *International Security*, Vo 33, No (Summer 2008), 82- 7, http://be fercenter ksg harvard edu/f es/IS330 _pp082- 7_Ta madge pdf; W am D O Ne and Ca t n Ta madge, "Correspondence: Costs and D ff cu t es of C os ng the Stra t of Hormuz," *International Security*, Vo 33, No 3 (W nter 2008/09), 90- 98, http://dspace m t edu /openaccess-d ssem nate/ 72 /57443

[0] Matthew Lev tt, *Hizballah and the Qods Force in Iran's Shadow War with the West*, Po cy Focus 23 (Wash ngton, D C : Wash ngton Inst tute, January 20 3), http://www wash ngton nst tute org/up oads/Documents/pubs/Po cyFocus 23 pdf

[ ] E senstadt, "M ss es and the Nuc ear Negot at ons w th Iran"

[2] Gareth Smyth, "New book on bas j he ps exp a n how Iran s hard ne fact on keeps country capt ve," *Guardian*, September 8, 20 5, http://www theguard an com/wor d/ ran-b og/20 5/sep/08/bas j-m t a-and-soc a -contro - n- ran-book- nterv ew

[3] A A foneh, "The Bas j Res stance Force," n Rob n Wr ght (Ed), *The Iran Primer*, (Wash ngton DC, Un ted States Inst tute for Peace: 20 0), http:// ranpr mer us p org/resource/bas j-res stance-force; A A foneh, "The Bas j Res stance Force: A Weak L nk n the Iran an Reg me?" Wash ngton Inst tute for Near East Po cy, *PolicyWatch* 627 February 5, 20 0, http://www wash ngton nst tute org/temp ateC05 php?CID 7 ; A A foneh, *What do Structural Changes in the Revolutionary Guards Mean?* Amer can Enterpr se Inst tute, M dd e Eastern Out ook No 7, September 2008, at: http://www ae org/docL b/20080923_23487MEO07_g pdf

[4] A foneh, *What Do Structural Changes in the Revolutionary Guards Mean?*

[ ] Thus, IRGC Navy commander Rear Adm ra A Fadav stated n Feb uary 20 4 that as a resu t of ts "awareness of the Is am c Repub c of Iran s deterrence capab ty… (the U S) announced that t w not enter a ground war w th n the next twenty years and (that) future Amer can wars w

take shape n the cyber and nava d mens ons " Am r Toumaj, Iran News Round Up, Februa y 0, 20 4, http://www cr t ca threats org/ ran-news -roundup/ ran-news-round-February- 0-20 4

⁵⁶ Mark C ayton, "Cyber-War: In Deed and Des re, Iran Emerg ng as a Major Power," *Christian Science Monitor*, March 6, 20 4, http://www csmon tor com/Wor d/Passcode/20 4/03 6/Cyber-war-In-deed-and-des re-Iran-emerg ng-as-a-major-power; Stuart McC ure, *Operation Cleaver* (Cy ance, December 20 4), http://www cy ance com/assets/C eaver/Cy ance_Operat on_C eaver_Repo t pdf; Na t V eneuve, Ned Moran, Thouf que Haq, and M ke Scott, *Operation Saffron Rose 2013* (F reEye, May 3, 20 4), https://www f reeye com/b og/threat -research/20 4/05/operat on-saffron-rose htm

⁵⁷ For more on th s component of Iran s deterrence posture, see: Gho am Reza Ja a , cha rman of the IRI s Pass ve Defense Organ zat on and former IRGC commander quoted n Y Mansharof and A Savyon, "Iran n Preparat ons, Dep oyment to W thstand Poss b e Attack by West," MEMRI Inqu ry and Ana ys s Ser es Report No 45 , Ju y 3, 2008, http://www memr org/report/en/0/0/0/0/0/0/2743 htm

⁵⁸ Yaakov Lapp n, "Ahmad nejad: Iran now Nuc ear Power," *YnetNews.com*, 20 December 2006, http://www ynetnews com/a t c es/0,7340,L -3342489,00 htm

⁵⁹ Thomas Erdbr nk, "Ayato ah Says Iran W   Contro Nuc ear A ms," Feb uary 6, 20 3, *New York Times*, http://www nyt mes com/20 3/02/ 7 /wor d/m dd eeast/supreme- eader-says- ran-not-seek ng-nuc ear-arms htm ?_r 0

⁶⁰ Mary Jordan and Kar V ck, "Wor d Leaders Condemn Iran an s Ca to W pe Israe 'Off the Map ," *Washington Post*, October 28, 2005, http://www wash ngtonpost com/wp-dyn/content/art c e/2005/ 0/27/AR2005 0270222 htm Iran s acknow edgement that a feas b ty study that the IAEA had obta ned from a fore gn nte gence se v ce n 2005 (and wh ch had apparent y or g nated n Iran) appeared to be that of a nuc ear warhead, wh e deny ng that t had come from Iran, may kew se have been ca cu ated to fu ther th s po cy of amb gu ty about Iran an ntent ons Yoss Me man, "Beh nd the scenes of UN nuc ear nspect on of Iran," *Haaretz*, October 22, 20 0, http://www haaretz com/weekend/week-s end /beh nd-the-scenes-of-un-nuc ear- nspect on-of- ran- 320599

⁶ Mark Land er and Dav d E Sanger, "C nton Speaks of Sh e d ng M deast From Iran," *New York Times*, Ju y 22, 2009, http://www nyt mes com /2009/07/23/wor d/as a/23d p o htm

⁶² A A foneh, Iran News Round Up, September 24, 20 2, http://www rantracker org/roundup/ ran-news-round-september-24-20 2

⁶³ Recent examp es nc ude c a ms that Iran had produced ts own "stea th f ghter" (wh ch proved to be a wooden mockup) and that t p anned to bu d nuc ear submar nes and a rcraft carr ers "Defense Off c a : Qah r-3 3 Home Made F ghter Jet to Protect Pers an Gu f," *Fars News Agency*, Apr 6, 20 3, http://eng sh farsnews com/newstext php?nn 9 07 6 450; "Iran P ans to Bu d Nuc ear-Fue ed Submar nes," *Fars News Agency*, June 2, 20 2, http://eng sh farsnews com/newstext php?nn 9 0308 864; "Commander: Iran P ans to Bu d A rcraft Carr ers," *Fars News Agency*, September 28, 20 , http://eng sh farsnews com/newstext php?nn 9007040435

⁶⁴ Tarem , "Iran an Strateg c Cu ture," 5- 8

⁶⁵ Adamsky, *Soviet, Russian, and Israeli Assessments of Iran's Nuclear Strategic Culture*, 47-48

⁶⁶ Iran an sources genera y use "soft powe " n a doub e sense, depend ng on context, to refer to that e ement of nat ona power that re es on non-m ta y nstruments, or that nf uences by the power of attract on as opposed to coerc on or nducements The atter conforms to the def n t on proposed by Joseph Nye For a br ef overv ew of the atter approach, see: Joseph Nye, "Th nk Aga n: Soft Power," *ForeignPolicy.com*, February 23, 2006, at: http://www fore gnpo cy com/art c es/2006/02/22/th nk_aga n_soft_power

⁶⁷ W Fu ton, Iran News Round Up, AEI, February 2 , 20 3, http://www rantracker org/ ran-news-round-february-2 -20 3

⁶⁸ "U S Off c a Says Iran Re y ng On 'Soft Power To Inf uence Iraq," *RFE/RL* Report, January 26, 20 , http://www rfer org/content/us _off c a _ ran_soft_power_ nf uence_ raq/2287522 htm

[69] Hamd Ma k and Maysam Behravesh, "Is Iran Creat ng ts Own State W th n Iraq?" Tehran Bureau, *The Guardian*, May 8, 20 5, http:/www theguard an com/wor d/20 5/may/ 8/ rans-state-w th n-state- n- raq-sh a

[70] Ib d

[7] "A L on n W nter: The Intr gu ng Ec pse of a M tary Hero, ' *Economist*, September 5, 20 5, http://www econom st com/news/m dd e-east -and-afr ca/2 663234- ntr gu ng-ec pse-m ta y-hero- on-w nter

[72] Matthew Lev tt and Ph p Smyth, Kata b a -Imam A , "Portra t of an Iraq Sh te M tant Group F ght ng ISIS," The Wash ngton Inst tute for Near East Po cy, *PolicyWatch* 2352, January 5, 20 5, http://www wash ngton nst tute org/po cy-ana ys s/v ew/kata b-a- mam-a -portra t-of-an - raq -sh te-m tant-group-f ght ng- s s

[73] Thus, fo ow ng the fa of Mosu to IS n June 20 4, sen or IRGC off cer Br g Gen Massoud Jazayer stated that "Iran has to d Iraq off c a s t s ready to prov de them w th… the same w nn ng strategy used n Syr a to put the terror sts on the defens ve Th s same strategy s now tak ng shape n Iraq - mob z ng masses of a ethn c groups " Mehrdad Ba a , "Iran genera says ready to he p Iraq aga nst m tants," *Reuters*, J ne 29, 20 4, http:// n reuters com/a t c e/20 4/06/29/uk- raq-secur ty- ran- dINKBN0F407R20 40629

[74] Syr a s Nat ona Defense Force, however, wh ch nc udes Chr st ans and pro-reg me Sunn s, s more d verse n compos t on than these other arge y Sh te m t as A A foneh,"Sh te Combat Casua t es Show the Depth of Iran s Invo vement n Syr a," The Wash ngton Inst tute for Near East Po cy, *PolicyWatch* 2458, August 3, 20 5, http://www wash ngton nst tute org/po cy-ana ys s/v ew/sh te-combat-casua t es-show-the-depth -of- rans- nvo vement- n-syr a; Ph p Smyth, "Iran s Afghan Sh te F ghters n Syr a," *PolicyWatch* 2262, The Wash ngton Inst tute for Near East Po cy, June 3, 20 4, http://www wash ngton nst tute org/po cy-ana ys s/v ew/ rans-afghan-sh te-f ghters- n-syr a

[7] Ph p Smyth, *The Shiite Jihad in Syria and its Regional Effects*, The Wash ngton Inst tute for Near East Po cy, Po cy Focus No 3 , 20 5, http://www wash ngton nst tute org/po cy-ana ys s/v ew/the-sh te-j had- n-syr a-and- ts-reg ona -effects

[76] Mehd Kha aj , "The Iran an C ergy s S ence," *Current Trends in Islamist Ideology*, vo 0, posted on ne on Ju y 2, 20 0, http://www currenttrends org/research/deta /the- ran an-c ergy s-s ence; Mehd Kha aj , *The Last Marja Sistani and the End of Traditional Religious Authority in Shiism*, The Wash ngton Inst tute for Near East Po cy, Po cy Focus No 59, September 2006, pp 6- , 25-3 , http://www wash ngton nst tute org/pubPDFs/Po cyFocus59f na pdf

[77] Hassan Rouhan speech to sen or IRGC off cers quoted n W Fu ton and Am r Toumaj, Iran News Round Up, September 6, 20 3, http://www rantracker org/ ran-news-round-september- 6-20 3

[78] M chae S ackman, "Iraq T es to Iran Create New R sks for Wash ngton," *New York Times*, June 8, 2006, http://www nyt mes com/2006/06/08 /wor d/m dd eeast/08 ran htm ?fta y

[79] E senstadt, Kn ghts, and A , *Iranian Influence in Iraq*, 2- 3

[80] Th s d scuss on on soft power s based arge y on: M chae E senstadt, "The L m ts of Iran s Soft Powe " n Rob n Wr ght (Ed) *The Iran Primer* B og, Un ted States Inst tute for Peace, March 22, 20 , http:// ranpr mer us p org/b og/a /M chae %20E senstadt See a so E senstadt, Kn ghts, and A , *Iranian Influence in Iraq*

[8] Except for a per od after the 2006 Lebanon War when H zba ah and Iran were very popu ar on the Arab street James Zoghby, "The Arab and Iran an D sconnect," *The World Post*, November 29, 20 4, http://www huff ngtonpost com/james-zoghby/the-arab-and- ran an-d sconnect_b_6240264 htm ; E senstadt, Kn ghts, and A , *Iran's Influence in Iraq Countering Tehran's Whole-of-Government Approach*, 5- 7

[82] For more on the nuc ear *fatwa* and ts m tat ons (s nce t can a ways be supp anted by a contra y *fatwa* f c rcumstances change, or overr dden f the "exped ency of the reg me" so requ res) see: M chae E senstadt and Mehd Kha aj , "Forget the Fatwa," *The National Interest*, March 4, 20 3, http://nat ona nterest org/commentary/forget-the-fatwa-8220; M chae E senstadt and Mehd Kha aj , *Nuclear Fatwa Religion and Politics in Iran's*

Proliferation Strategy, Po cy Focus No   5, September 20 , http://www wash ngton nst tute org/po cy-ana ys s/v ew/nuc ear-fatwa-re g on -and-po t cs- n- rans-pro ferat on-strategy

[83] Is am c Repub c News Agency, October 9, 988

[84] U S Depa tment of State, *Condition (10)(C) Report Compliance with the Convention on the Prohibition of the Development, Production, Stockpiling and Use of Chemical Weapons and on Their Destruction*, Apr   5, 20 5, http://www state gov/t/avc/r s/rpt/20 5/243245 htm

[8] Dav d A br ght, "Iran s Noncomp ance w th Its Internat ona Atom c Energy Agency Ob gat ons," test mony, House Subcomm ttee on the M dd e East and North Afr ca, Comm ttee on Fore gn Affa rs, March 24, 20 5, http://fore gnaffa rs house gov/hear ng/subcomm ttee-hear ng- ran -s-noncomp ance- ts- nternat ona -atom c-energy-agency-ob gat ons; Pau K Kerr, *Iran's Nuclear Program Tehran's Compliance with International Obligations*, Report R40094 (Congress ona Research Serv ce, Apr   28, 20 4), http://fas org/sgp/crs/nuke/R40094 pdf

[86] Dan e Sa sbury and Ian J Stewa t, *Valves for Arak Proliferation Case Study Series*, Project A pha Centre for Sc ence and Secur ty Stud es (London: K ng s Co ege, August 22, 20 4), https://www acsss nfo/pro ferat on/ tem/342-va ves-for-arak; Ian J Stewart and N ck G ard, *Sabotage? Iranian Exhibition Gives Insights into Illicit Procurement Methods and Challenges*, Project A pha Centre for Sc ence and Secur ty Stud es (London: K ng s Co ege, September 8, 20 4), https://www acsss nfo/pro ferat on/ tem/347-sabotage- ran an-exh b t on-g ves- ns ghts - nto- c t-procurement-methods-and-cha enges

[87] A br ght, "Iran s Noncomp ance w th Its Internat ona Atom c Energy Agency Ob gat ons"

[88] IAEA Board of Governors, *Implementation of the NPT Safeguards Agreement and Relevant Provisions of Security Council Resolutions in the Islamic Republic of Iran*, November 8, 20 , https://www aea org/s tes/defau t/f es/gov20 -65 pdf; Joby Warr ck, "Iran May Have Cont nued Weapons Research after 2003, IAEA Ch ef Says," *Washington Post*, Apr 8, 20 3, https://www wash ngtonpost com/wor d/nat ona -secur ty/ ran -may-have-cont nued-weapons-research- aea-ch ef-says/20 3/04/08/002 a9e0-a066- e2-82bc-5 538ae90a4_sto y htm

[89] A br ght, "Iran s Noncomp ance w th Its Internat ona Atom c Energy Agency Ob gat ons"

[90] *After Liberation Came Destruction Iraqi Militias and the Aftermath of Amerli*, Human R ghts Watch, March 8, 20 5, https://www hrw org /repo t/20 5/03/ 8/after- berat on-came-destruct on/ raq -m t as-and-aftermath-amer ; *Ruinous Aftermath: Militias Abuses Following Iraq's Recapture rit*, Human R ghts Watch, September 20, 20 5, https://www h w org/report/20 5/09/20/ru nous-aftermath/m t as-abuses-fo ow ng - raqs-recapture-t kr t

[9] Ya da Hak m, "Syr a footage sheds ght on Iran s nvo vement," *BBC News* M dd e East, October 30, 20 3, http://www bbc com/news/wor d -m dd e-east-24748 43?STh sFB

[92] A foneh,"Sh te Combat Casua t es Show the Depth of Iran s Invo vement n Syr a"; A A foneh, "Max ma Exposure, M n ma Presence: Iran s M ta y Engagement n Iraq," The Wash ngton Inst tute for Near East Po cy, *PolicyWatch* 2477, August 25, 20 5, http://www wash ngton nst tute org/po cy-ana ys s/v ew/max ma -exposure-m n ma -presence- rans-m tary-engagement- n- raq

[93] Dav d A br ght, Pau Brannan, and Andrea Str cker, *Has Iran initiated a slow motion breakout to a nuclear weapon?* ISIS Report, Ju y 2, 20 0, http:// s s-on ne org/ s s-repo ts/deta /has- ran- n t ated-a-s ow-mot on-breakout-to-a-nuc ear-weapon/8

[94] M chae Rub n, *Into the Shadows Radical Vigilantes in Khatami's Iran* (Wash ngton, DC: The Wash ngton Inst tute for Near East Po cy, 200)

[9] Thus, accord ng to one m d-rank ng scho ar, Hojjato Is am Mohammad Bagher Zadeh, "Our success has been due pr mar y to asymmetr c warfare The enemy has weapons of mass destruct on, but we w w n due to our asymmetr c wa fare We have God, they have b o og ca weapons We have the even ng prayer, they have chem ca weapons Th s has been shown by the 33-day war [e , the 2006 Lebanon War], and the 8-year war [e , the Iran-Iraq War] Our approach s f ght ng asymmetr c wars, t s not because of nuc ear weapons, but because of deo ogy, mora ty, and sp r tua ty n our schoo of thought " Quoted n Steven D tto, *Nuclear Weapons in Iranian Religious Discourse*, March 24, 20 3, p 5,

Michael Eisenstadt

https://se fscho ar f es wordpress com/20 3/03/ rand scourse5 pcf

[96] Thus, nava m nes a d by Iran dur ng the atter phases of ts war w th Iraq bore Iran an mark ngs, wh e weapons that Iran sent to Iraq spec a groups to be used aga nst Amer can so d ers there, st bore the manufacturer s data p ates, wh ch nd cated the p ace and date of manufacture n Iran It seems that n each case, Tehran d d not care whether the US knew the or g ns of these weapons, and may have even re shed the opportun ty to st ck the r thumb n Amer ca s eyes

[97] Lev tt, *Hezbollah,* 22-48 See a so D Peterson et a v The Is am c Repub c of Iran, M n stry of Fore gn Affa rs and the M n st y of Informat on and Secur ty, Un ted States D str ct Court, D str ct of Co umb a, Docket No CA 0 -2684, March 7, 2003

[98] Lev tt, *Hezbollah,* 75- 6; B anford, *Warriors of God,* 97, 98, 5; Byman, *A High Price,* 222-224

[99] Lev tt, *Hezbollah,* 75- 6; B anford, *Warriors of God,* 5; Byman, *A High Price,* 222-224

[00] Lev tt, *Hezbollah,* 8 -207; Kenneth Po ack, *The Persian Puzzle The Conflict Between Iran and America* (New York: Random House, 2004), 273-275, 282; Lou s J Freeh, "Khobar Towers," *Wa'l Street Journal,* June 23, 2006, http://www wsj com/art c es/SB 5 0270256878833 ; USA v Ahmed a -Mughass et a , Ind ctment, US D str ct Court, Eastern D str ct of VA, A exandr a, VA, No 0 -228-A, June 200

[0] O ver Tree, "Egypt Fo ed Second Iran an P ot to K Saud Ambassador: Reports," *International Business Times,* May , 20 2, http://www bt mes com/egypt-fo ed-second- ran ar-p ot-k -saud -ambassador-reports-694029; Dav d Ignat us, "Inte gence L nks Iran to Saud D p omat s Murder," *Washington Post,* October 3, 20 , http://www wash ngtonpost com/b ogs/post-pa t san/post/ nte gence- nks- ran-to-saud -d p omats-murder/20 / 0/ 3/gIQAFzCP L_b og htm

[02] Sh mon Shap ra, "The Or g ns of H zba ah," *Jerusalem Quarterly,* no 46 (Spr ng 988), 5 30; Azadeh Moaven , "Hard-L ners n Iran Worry about U S Inf uence n Iraq," *Los Angeles Times,* Apr , 2003, http://art c es at mes com/2003/apr/ /news/war-sp ts ; Ned Parker, Raheem Sa man, and Saad Fakhr deen, "Dread Descends on Iraq Ho y C ty," *Los Angeles Times,* Apr 20, 2008, http://a t c es at mes com/2008/apr/20 /wor d/fg-najaf20 Lam was a notor ous Sadr C ty spec a group eader who sp t from the Mahd Army and was be eved respons b e for the torture and death of thousands of c v ans n 2006 2007; see J n Swa n, "Is Th s Iraq s Most Pro f c Mass K er?" *Times* (London), January 2 , 2007, http://www t meson ne co uk/to /news/wor d/a t c e 294957 ece?token nu &offset 0&page

[03] Bruce R ede , "The Myster ous Re at onsh p between a -Qa da and Iran," *CTC Sentinel,* Ju y 3, 20 0, https://www ctc usma edu/posts/the -myster ous-re at onsh p-between-a -qa da-and- ran; Dan e L Byman, "Un ke y A ance: Iran s Secret ve Re at onsh p w th A -Qaeda," *IHS Defense* R sk and Secur ty Consu t ng, Ju y 20 2, http://www brook ngs edu/research/art c es/20 2/07/ ran-a -qaeda-byman

[04] E senstadt, Kn ghts, and A , *Iranian Influence in Iraq*

[0] A A foneh, Ahmad Maj dyar, and M chae Rub n (eds), Iran News Round-Up, Februa y 8, 20 2, http://www rantracker org/roundup/ ran -news-round-februa y-8-20 2

[06] La a Bassam, "Iran cou d str ke U S bases f Israe attacks: H zba ah," *Reuters,* September 4, 20 2, http://www reuters com /a t c e/20 2/09/04/us- ebanon-hezbo ah- srae - dUSBRE882 KU20 20904

[07] M chae E senstadt and M chae Kn ghts, *Beyond Worst-Case Analysis Iran's Likely Responses to an Israeli Preventive Strike,* Wash ngton Inst tute Po cy Note No , June 20 2, http://www wash ngton nst tute org/po cy-ana ys s/v ew/beyond-worst-case-ana ys s- rans- ke y-responses -to-an- srae -prevent ve

[08] B Sam , "Iran: Int fada Conference n Tehran has Mu t p e Object ves," *RFE/RL,* Apr 4, 2006, http://www fer org/content /a t c e/ 067669 htm

[09] B Sam , "M dd e East: Iran an 'Vo unteers to He p H zba ah," *RFE/RL,* Ju y 3 , 2006, http://www fer org/content/art c e/ 070228 htm ; J m Sc utto, "Ins de Iran: F nd ng 'Vo unteers to F ght Israe ," *ABC News,* August 4, 2006, http://abcnews go com/WNT/story? d 2275230; M chae

S ackman, "Iran G ves Hamas Enthus ast c Support, but D screet y, Just n Case," *New York Times*, Janua y 3, 2009, http://www nyt mes com/2009 /0 / 3/wor d/m dd eeast/ 3 ran htm ?_r 0

[0] Mehd Jed n a, "Tehran F nds Neat Way Out on Gaza Sh pment," *Mianeh*, Ju y 3, 20 0, http://m aneh net/a t c e/tehran-f nds-neat-way-out-gaza -sh pment

"Attack on Syr a, Str ke on Iran and A es: Ve ayat ," *Press TV*, January 26, 20 3, http://www presstv r/deta /20 3/0 /26/285606/attack ng-syr a - s-attack ng- ran-ve ayat /

[2] "Iran Refused Assad s Request to H t Back at Israe ," *Times of Israel*, February 4, 20 3, http://www t mesof srae com/ ran-reported y-refuses -assad-request-to-h t-back-at- srae /

[3] Anshe Pfeffer, "Hezbo ah 'Refused Hamas Request to Bomb Israe n Gaza War ," *Haaretz*, November 0, 20 0, http://www haaretz com/pr nt -ed t on/news/hezbo ah-refused-hamas-request-to-bomb- srae - n-gaza-war- 323862; "Hamas appea s d rect y to Hezbo ah eader to he p f ght Israe , Nasra ah un ke y to y e d to pressure to send f ghters," *An-Nahar*, Ju y 30, 20 4, http://en annahar com/art c e/ 56003-hamas-appea s -d rect y-to-hezbo ah- eadah- eader-to-he p-f ght- srae -nasra ah

[4] In a Fab an strategy, fronta attacks and dec s ve batt e s avo ded and v cto y s atta ned by wear ng down the enemy through attr t on, nd rect on, and demora zat on The name s der ved from the Roman po t c an and genera Fab us Max mus, who pract ced such an approach aga nst the Ca thag n an genera Hann ba n Ita y dur ng the Second Pun c War (2 8-202 BCE) For more on Fab us Max mus, see B H L dde Hart, *Strategy* (New York: S gnet, 974), 3- 4, 26-27, 29-30, 59

"Ch ef Iran an Nuc ear Affa rs Negot ator Hose n Musav an: The Negot at ons w th Europe Bought Us T me to Comp ete the Esfahan UCF Project and the Work on the Centr fuges n Natanz," MEMRI Spec a D spatch No 957, August 2, 2005, http://www memr tv org/report/en / 439 htm

[6] Po ack, *The Persian Puzzle*, 273-275, 282

[7] Gerhard Bower ng, "The Concept of T me n Is am," Proceed ngs of the Amer can Ph osoph ca Soc ety, Vo 4 , No , 997; Gerhard Bower ng, "Ideas of T me n Pers an Suf sm," *Journal of Persian Studies*, vo 30, 992, pp 77-89; Zakar ya Wr ght, "L v ng n T me: Mus ms and the Modern T me-Crunch," *Islam America*, February 0, 2008, http://www s amamer ca org/A t c eL brary /L v ng nT meMus msandtheModernT meCrunch aspx

[8] Ehsan Yarshater, "The Pers an Presence n the Is am c Wor d," n R chard G Hovann s an and Georges Sabagh, *The Persian Presence in the Islamic World* (Cambr dge Un vers ty Press: 998), 4- 25; R chard Frye, *The Golden Age of Persia* (London, Phoen x Press: 975), 50- 74; Bernard Lew s, "Iran n H sto y," ecture at Sack er Inst tute of Advanced Stud es, Te Av v Un vers ty, Janua y 8, 999, - 2

[9] Ruho ah K Ramazan , *Revolutionary Iran Challenge and Response in the Middle East* (Ba t more, MD: Johns Hopk ns Un vers ty Press, 988), 3- 8

[20] M chae E senstadt, *What Iran's Chemical Past Tells Us About its Nuclear Future*, Research Note No 4, The Wash ngton Inst tute, Apr 20 4, 2, http://www wash ngton nst tute org/up oads/Documents/pubs/ResearchNote 7_E senstadt2 pdf

[2] "Israe Warsh ps Cross Suez Cana Aga n," *Haaretz*, Ju y 4, 2009, http://www haaretz com/news/ srae -warsh ps-cross-suez-cana -aga n 279983; Isabe Kershner, "Israe S ent as Iran an Sh ps Trans t Suez Cana ," *New York Times*, February 22, 20 , http://www nyt mes com/20 /02 /23/wor d/m dd eeast/23suez htm ; "Iran to Send F eet of Warsh ps to Red Sea, Med terranean Sea," *Fars News Agency*, January 23, 20 , http://eng sh farsnews com/newstext php?nn 89 03 40

[22] Thomas Erdbr nk, "At Iran Nuc ear Summ t, Ahmad nejad Ca s for U S to D sarm F rst," *Washington Post*, Apr 7, 20 0, http://www wash ngtonpost com/wp-dyn/content/art c e/20 0/04/ 7/AR20 004 702   htm ?hp d topnews

[23] "Defense M n ster Inspect on of Iran an Cargo Sh ps Imper s R g ona Secur ty," *Fars News Agency*, June 30, 20 0, http://eng sh farsnews com /newstext php?nn 890409 475

[24] M chae E senstadt, *Not by Sanctions Alone Using Military and Other Means to Bolster Nuclear Diplomacy with Iran* (Wash ngton Inst tute, 20 3), 9-30, http://www wash ngton nst tute org/up oads/Docurnents/pubs/Strateg cReport 3_E senstadt2 pdf

[2] Speech by A Khamene , Imam A M tary Academy, October , 20 , http://eng sh khamene r/ ndex php?opt on com _content&task v ew& d 558&Item d 4; Speech by A Khamene , Imam Reza s Shr ne, March 20, 20 2, http://eng sh khamene r// ndex php?opt on com_content&task v ew& d 620&Item d 4

[26] A good examp e of Iran s embrace of doub e standards wh en t serves ts own nterests s the nuc ear dea w th the P5+ /EU (th Jo nt Comprehens ve P an of Act on or JCPOA) wh ch n add t on to estab sh ng a number of precedents unfavorab e to Tehran wh ch t accepted on y re uctant y estab shed a number of precedents favorab e to t n order to ga n ts buy- n

[27] Adamsky, *Soviet, Russian, and Israeli Assessments of Iran's Nuclear Strategic Culture*, 48

[28] Thomas L Fr edman, *From Beirut to Jerusalem* (New York: Farrar, Straus & G roux, 989), 76- 05

[29] The reg me ke y a so feared that a fronta c ash w th the reform movement m ght have ed e ements n the secur ty forces to d sobey orders or jo n the oppos t on, caus ng the secur ty forces to fracture M chae E senstadt, "The Secur ty Forces of the Is am c Repub c and the Fate of the Oppos t on," The Wash ngton Inst tute for Near East Po cy, *Po cyWatch* 538, June 9, 2009, http://www wash ngton nst tute org/tem-p ateC05 php?CID 3076

[30] M chae E senstadt, *Iran's Islamic Revolution Lessons for the Arab Spring of 2011*, Nat ona Defense Un vers ty, Strateg c Forum No 267, Apr 20 , http://www ndu edu/ nss/docUp oaded/SF%20267_E senstadt pdf

[3] A Ahmad Mot agh, "Po t ca Pr soners and the Secur ty Apparatus n Post-E ect on Iran," *Muftah*, August 2, 20 0, http://muftah org/ p 2 5

[32] *A Brief History of "House Arrests" and Detentions in "Safe Houses" What Will Be the Fate of Disappeared Leaders?* Internat ona Campa gn for Human R ghts n Iran, March 6, 20 , http://www ranhumanr ghts org/20 /03/h story-of-house-arrests/

[33] Shahram Chub n, "Command and Contro n a Nuc ear Armed Iran," IFRI Secur ty Stud es Center, *Proliferation Papers*, No 45, January- February 20 3, http://www fr org/en/pub cat ons/enotes/pro ferat on-papers/command-and-contro -nuc ear-armed- ran

[34] Mark Bowden, *Guests of the Ayatollah—The Iran Hostage Crisis The First Battle in America's War with Militant Islam* (New York, Grove Press: 2006), 8- 5

[3] Cr st, *Gulf of Conflict*, 25-26

[36] Am r Toumaj and John Lesnew ch, Iran News Round Up, AEI Cr t ca Threats Project, January 27, 20 4, http://www cr t ca threats org/ ran-news -roundup/ ran-news-round-january-27-20 4

[37] In th s regard, Tehran s approach s s m ar to that of j had st groups such as H zba ah, Hamas, a -Qaeda, and the Ta ban See Thomas E kjer N ssen, *The Taliban's Information Warfare A Comparative Analysis of NATO Information Operations (Info Ops) and Taliban Information Activities*, Roya Dan sh Defence Co ege Br ef (January 2008), 7

[38] Th s s not a un que y Is am c way of th nk ng about war In the Jew sh B b e, when Dav d cha enged the heav y-armed and -armored warr or Go ath w th on y h s s ng and a st ck, the Ph st ne g ant scorns h m, say ng: "Am I a dog that you come aga nst me w th st cks?" To wh ch Dav d responded: "You come aga nst me w th sword and spear and jave n; but I come aga nst you n the name of the Lord of Hosts, the God of the arm es of Israe , whom you have taunted Th s day the Lord w de ver you nto my hands " (Samue I, 7:45-47) There are many other accounts n the B b e that ref ect th s wor dv ew L kew se, W am Shakespeare n Henry V (Act 4, Scene 8) has the k ng order h s troops after the r ops d d v c-

tory at Ag ncou t to forswear cred t for the r success, and to thank God for the r v cto y by s ng ng Psa m   5: "Not unto us, O Lord, not to us, but to Your name g ve g ory "

[39] Maz ar Bahar , "   8 Days, 2 Hours, 54 M nutes," *Newsweek*, November 30, 2009, http://www newsweek com/2009/   /2 / 8-days- 2-hours -54-m nutes htm

[40] Abraham an, "The Parano d Sty e n Iran an Po t cs,"   - 3

[4] "IRGC Ch ef Warns of Cu tura Threats," *Press TV*, June 9, 20 0, http://www presstv r/deta / 29769 htm See a so the statements by Jafar n W Fu ton, Iran News Round Up, AEI Iran Tracker, February 28, 20 3, http://www rantracker org/ ran-news-round-februa y-28-20 3

[42] "Iran an State TV Acts as an Arm of the Inte gence Apparatus," Internat ona Campa gn for Human R ghts n Iran, August   , 20 0, http://www ranhumanr ghts org/20 0/08/ ran an-state-tv-acts-as-an-arm-of-the- nte gence-apparatus/

[43] Anonymous, "Iran s War Aga nst Western Cu ture: Never End ng, A ways Los ng," PBS Tehran Bureau, December   , 20 , http://www pbs org/wgbh/pages/front ne/tehranbureau/20 / 2/med a-the-reg mes-war-aga nst-western-cu ture-never-end ng-a ways - os ng htm # xzz3QXr C6 C

[44] Kar m Sadjadpour, *Reading Khamenei The World View of Iran's Most Powerful Leader* (Wash ngton, DC: Carneg e Endowment for Internat ona Peace, 2008), 7

[4] Mahmood Enayat, *Satellite Jamming in Iran A War Over Airwaves*, A Sma Med a Report, November 20 2, http://sma med a org uk/s tes /defau t/f es/Sate te%20Jamm ng pdf; Ana Cardenes, The Internet n Iran, a da y st ugg e aga nst censorsh p, IANS/EFE, October 2, 20 4; L k ng Facebook n Tehran: Soc a Network ng n Iran, Iran Med a Program, Annenberg Schoo for Commun cat ons, Un vers ty of Pennsy van a, 20 4, http://www ranmed aresearch org/en/research/down oad/ 609; S murgh A yan, Homa Aryan, and J A ex Ha derman, Internet Censorsh p n Iran: A F rst Look, Proceed ngs of the 3rd USENIX Workshop on Free and Open Commun cat on on the Internet, August 20 3; Cormac Ca anan et a , Leap ng Over the F rewa : A Rev ew of Censorsh p C rcumvent on Too s, Freedom House, 20 0, https://freedomhouse org/s tes/defau t/f es / n ne_ mages/Censorsh p pdf See a so, M chae P zz , "Iran government m n ster: Med a bans may seem ' aughab e n 5 years," *Aljazeera America*, December 9, 20 3, http://amer ca a jazeera com/art c es/20 3/ 2/ 9/ ran an-m n stermed abansmayseem aughab e n5years htm

[46] Khamene has repeated y argued aga nst comprom se w th the US, c a m ng th s wou d be seen as weakness that wou d on y nv te add t ona pressure and demands Sadjadpour, *Reading Khamenei*, 6

[47] Ehud Yaar , "The Muqawama Doctr ne," *Jerusalem Report*, November 3, 2006

[48] See, for nstance, the nfograph c on the Supreme Leaders webs te regard ng the ach evements of Iran s po cy of nuc ear res stance, http://eng sh khamene r// ndex php?opt on com_content&task v ew& d 637

[49] The dea that conf ct may serve soc a and po t ca funct ons a so has a ong trad t on n Western soc a sc ence Georg S mme , *Conflict and the Web of Group-Affiliations* (New York, Free Press: 955); Lew s Coser, *The Functions of Social Conflict* (New York, Free Press: 956)

[0] For more on the cata yt c effect of the 40-day Mus m mourn ng per od on the esca at ng cyc e of v o ence dur ng the revo ut on, see: Gary S ck, *All Fall Down America's Tragic Encounter with Iran* (New York: Random House, 985), 34-35

The IRI has at t mes been concerned that the oss of revo ut onary zea has underm ned the re ab ty of the IRGC, ever s nce Revo ut onary Guard un ts refused to quash r ots n the town of Qazv n n 994 These concerns were re nforced by reports that IRGC personne voted n 997 for reform st pres dent a cand date Mohammad Khatam n even greater proport ons than d d the genera popu at on (73 versus 69 percent) Th s vot ng pattern nd cates that the IRGC rank and f e ref ected the d v s ons w th n Iran an soc ety Th s shou d not have come as a surpr se; for the past two decades, the IRGC has ncreas ng y come to re y on conscr pts to meet ts manpower needs, ra s ng doubts about ts re ab ty shou d t be needed to que unrest Even dur ng the Iran-Iraq War, the IRGC Navy cons sted of a m x of ded cated revo ut onar es, conscr pts, and mpressed deserters, and as a resu t, t often avo ded tak ng r sks wh e operat ng aga nst US nava forces n the Pers an Gu f Cr st, *Gulf of Conflict*, 5

[2] Contend ng approaches to wa f ght ng kew se ex st n the arm ed forces of the IRI, where the debate concerns the re at ve va ue of re g ous zea and techn ca competence The regu ar m tary has tended to em race a more trad t ona approach to war, w th a re at ve y ba anced emph as s on hardware, techno ogy, and the human e ement Its force structure, wh ch resemb es those of most Western arm es, ref ects th s fact By contrast, the IRGC has e evated the mora and sp r tua d mens on above a oth ers n the be ef that fa th, deo og ca comm tment, and re g ous zea are the keys to v ctory Thus, the IRGC or g na y cons sted of poor y tra ned rregu ar mass nfantry forces that spec a zed n human wave attacks, though t eventua y estab shed quas -convent ona nfantry, armor, and a t ery format ons, as we as nava and a r arms dur ng the Iran-Iraq War The IRGC s approach came to dom nate Iran an th nk ng dur ng the Iran-Iraq War, though ts th nk ng has evo ved s nce then to ref ect a more ba anced apprec at on of the re at ve mpo tance of mora and techno og ca factors Nonethe ess, the IRGC does not a ways get the newest and most capab e systems n the IRI s nventory perhaps due to res dua skept c sm on ts part regard ng the mportance of techno ogy Steven Ward, "H stor ca Perspect ves on Iran s Way of War," Presentat on to the Wash ngton Inst tute for Near East Po cy, June 8, 2009; Far bo z Haghshenass, "Iran s A r Force: St ugg ng to Ma nta n Read ness," Wash ngton Inst tute for Near East Po cy, *PolicyWatch* 066, December 22, 2005, http://www wash ngton nst tute org/temp ateC05 php?CID 2422; Far borz Haghshenass, *Iran's Asymmetric Naval Warfare*

[3] Abbas Amanat, *Apocalyptic Islam and Iranian Shiism* (London: I B Taur s, 2009), 4 -70, 22 -25 ; Mehd Kha aj, Apoca ypt c Po t cs: On the Rat ona ty of Iran an Po cy, Po cy Focus No 79 (Wash ngton, D C : Wash ngton Inst tute, Janua y 2008), 3-6, 4- 8; A A foneh, "Ahm ad ne ad versus the C ergy," Amer can Enterpr se Inst tute, M dd e East Out ook, no 5 (August 2008), -4

[4] Jed n a, "Tehran F nds Neat Way Out on Gaza Sh pment"

Kev n Hechtkopf, "Panetta: Iran Cannot Deve op Nukes, B ock Stra t," *Face the Nation*, CBS News, Janua y 8, 20 2, http://www cbsnews com /830 -3460_ 62-57354645/panetta- ran-cannot-deve op-nukes-b ock-stra t /; E sabeth Bum er, Er c Schm tt and Thom Shanker, "U S Sends Top Iran an Leader a Warn ng on Stra t Threat," *New York Times*, Janu ary 2, 20 2, http://www nyt mes com/20 2/0 / 3/wor d/m dd eeast/us-warns- op - ran- eader-not-to-shut-stra t-of-hormuz htm ?_r 0

[6] "Iran Warns US Aga nst Send ng Back A rcraft Carr er to th e Pers an Gu f," *Fars News Agency*, Janua y 3, 20 2, http://eng sh2 farsnews com /newstext php?nn 9007270208; Rob n Pomeroy and Hashem Ka antar , "Iran Backs Off Warn ngs About U S Sh ps," *Reuters*, January 2 , 20 2 http://uk reuters com/art c e/20 2/0 /2 /uk- ran-usa- dUKTRE 0K0DG20 20 2

[7] Thom Shanker, "Iran Chases U S Drone over Pers an Gu f," *New York Times*, March 4, 20 3, http://www nyt mes com/20 3/03/ 5/wor d /m dd eeast/ ran-pursues-us-drone-over-pers an-gu f htm

[8] "Attack on Syr a, Str ke on Iran and A es: Ve ayat ," *Press TV*, January 26, 20 3, http://www presstv r/deta /20 3/0 /26/285606 attack ng -syr a- s-attack ng- ran-ve ayat /

[9] Kay Arm n Serjo e, "Iran Cha enges U S and Saud Arab a by Send ng A d Sh p to Rebe s n Yemen," *Time*, May 8, 20 5, http:// t me com /3882293/ ran-saud -a d-sh p/

[60] Off ce of the D rector of Nat ona Inte gence, *Iran Nuclear Intentions and Capabilities*, November 2007, http://graph cs8 nyt mes com /packages/pdf/ nternat ona /2007 203_re ease pdf; Joby Warr ck, "Iran May Have Cont nued Weapons Research after 2003, IAEA Ch ef Says," *Washington Post*, Apr 8, 20 3, https://www wash ngtonpost com/wor d/nat ona -secur ty/ ran-may-have-cont nued-weapons-research- aea-ch ef -says/20 3/04/08/002 a9e0-a066- e2-82bc-5 538ae90a4_s ory htm

[6] In the words of Rouhan , "Wh e we were ta k ng w th the Europeans n Tehran... by creat ng a ca m env ronment, we were ab e to comp ete the work [on the convers on fac ty] n Esfahan " Hassan Rouhan , 'Beyond the Cha enges Fac ng Iran and the IAEA Concern ng the Nuc ear Doss e ', *Rahbord*, September 30, 2005, as quoted n *Great Expectations Iran's New President and the Nuclear Talks*, Cr s s Group M dd e East Br ef ng No 36, August 3, 20 3, - 2, http://www cr s sgroup org/~/med a/F es/M dd e%20East%20North%20Afr ca/Iran%20Gu f Iran/b0 6 -great-expectat ons- rans-new-pres dent-and-the-nuc ear-ta ks pdf

[62] Instead, t avo ded the Israe red ne by convert ng ts stocks of 20-percent-enr ched uran um nto ox de form or fue p ates for a research reactor forms that wou d have requ red reconvers on (a t me-consum ng process) pr or to further enr chment

[63] In a December 20 2 news conference, IRGC Aerospace Force commander Br g Gen Am r A Haj zadeh stated that "We don t need m ss es w th over 2,000km but we have the techno ogy to bu d them," add ng that "Israe s our ongest-range target " "Commander Names Israe as Iran s Long-Range Target," *Fars News Agency*, December 0, 20 2, http://eng sh2 farsnews com/newstext php?nn 9 07 25969 L kew se, n a December 20 3 speech, IRGC commander Maj Gen Mohammad A Jafar stated that "We are st now ncreas ng the range of our m ss es, but current y the Supreme Leader has commanded that we m t the range of our m ss es to 2,000km " W Fu ton and Am r Toumaj, Iran News Round Up, December , 20 3, http://www rantracker org/ ran-news-round-december- -20 3

[64] Uz Rub n, "Showcase of M ss e Pro ferat on: Iran s M ss e and Space Program," *Arms Control Today*, Vo 42, No , January/February 20 2, https://www armscontro org/act/20 2_0 -02/Showcase_of_M ss e_Pro ferat on_Irans_M ss e_and_Space_Program

[6] Internat ona Atom c Energy Agency, *Implementation of the NPT Safeguards Agreement and Relevant Provisions of Security Council Resolutions in the Islamic Republic of Iran*, February 20, 20 4, https://www aea org/s tes/defau t/f es/gov20 4- 0 pdf

[66] Chr stopher De Be a gue, "Ta k L ke an Iran an," *The Atlantic*, September 20 2, http://www theat ant c com/magaz ne/arch ve/20 2/09/ta k - ke-an- ran an/309056/ It s not c ear how th s ack of concern w th cons stency affects how Iran an off c a s v ew statements by fore gn eaders In ght of the tendency of U S off c a s to ssue stern warn ngs that are not fo owed up on (e g , that a No th Korean nuc ear weapon wou d be "unacceptab e"), t s hard to avo d the conc us on that th s s someth ng of an Amer can hab t as we

[67] W am S Haas, "Pers an Psycho ogy," *Iran* (New York: Co umb a Un vers ty Press, 946), 6 36; W am O Beeman, "What Is (Iran an) Nat ona Character? A Soc o ngu st c Approach," *Iranian Studies* (W nter 976): 22 48, and; Graham Fu er, *The Center of the Universe The Geopolitics of Iran* (Bou der, CO: Westv ew Press, 99), 8 33

[68] IRGC Commander: War on Iran Tr ggers Wor d War III, *Fars News Agency*, September 23, 20 2, http://eng sh2 farsnews com /newstext php?nn 9 0624 874

[69] Patr ck C awson, "How Iran M ght Test a Nuc ear Accord Lessons from the Past: Report about a Wash ngton Inst tute for Near East Po cy Co oqu um," June 25, 20 5

[70] "Hagg ng Irked Russ ans," *Tehran Times International*, October 29, 20 0, http:// ran-t mes com/hagg ng- rked- uss ans/

[7] Matthew Bodner, "Underwhe m ng Bus ness Resu ts at MAKS A r Show, Defense News, August 29, 20 5, http://www defensenews com/story /defense/po cy-budget/warfare/20 5/08/29/underwhe m ng-bus ness-resu ts-maks-a r-show/7 323 30/

[72] There s a precedent for th s: the 2006 Israe -H zba ah war Between November 2005 and Ju y 2006, H zba ah attempted to k dnap Israe so d ers on at east f ve separate occas ons, and n each case, Israe s responded n a rather desu tory manner; when H zba ah f na y succeeded n k dnapp ng two Israe so d ers, Israe dec ared war and h t Lebanon w th a pun sh ng a r campa gn Afterward, H zba ah ch ef Hassan Nasra ah adm tted that had he known that the k dnapp ng wou d ead to war, he wou d not have ordered t Zeev Sch ff, "K dnap of So d ers n Ju y Was H zba ah s F fth Attempt," *Haaretz*, September 9, 2006, http://www haaretz com/news/k dnap-of-so d ers- n-ju y-was-hezbo ah-s-f fth-attempt - 97595

[73] Jay So omon and Ju an E Barnes, "U S We ghs a D rect L ne to Iran," *Wall Street Journal*, September 9, 20 , http://on ne wsj com/a t c e /SB 000 424053 9033740045765789907 87792046 htm ; Address by Adm ra Mu en to the Carneg e Endowment for Internat ona Peace, September 2 , 20 , http://carneg eendowment org/20 /09/20/adm ra -m ke-mu en/57gg; "Iran Rejects U S Hot ne Request," *Fars News Agency*, November , 20 2, http://eng sh farsnews com/newstext php?nn 9 07 8530

[74] Dan Rav v, "U S push ng Israe to stop assass nat ng Iran an nuc ear sc ent sts," *CBS News*, March , 20 4, http://www cbsnews com/news/us -push ng- srae -to-stop-assass nat ng- ran an-nuc ear-sc ent sts/

Michael Eisenstadt

7 For more on Iran an narrat ves of v ctory see: Adamsky, *Soviet, Russian, and Israeli Assessments of Iran's Nuclear Strategic Culture*, 8; Tarem "Iran an Strateg c Cu ture," 8

76 A s mart a prowess s of pa t cu ar mpo tance due to h s pre-em nent status n Sh te Is am (second on y to Muhammad) and the great mportance that Is am attaches to the power of persona examp e Thus, Is am c aw s based, n pa t, on the had th (the say ngs and act ons of the prophet Muhammad) wh e Sh tes are enjo ned to choose a sen o c er c to be the r marja (sources of emu at on) n matters of fa th

77 Reza Hagh ghatNejad, *What Does Khamenei Mean by "Heroic Flexibility?"* September 8, 20 3, http://en ranw re com/features/2687/; Arash Karam , "Ayato ah Khamene s 'Hero c F ex b ty'," *Al-Mon tor*, September 9, 20 3, http:// ranpu se a -mon tor com/ ndex php/20 3/09/285 /khamene s-hero c-f ex b ty/

78 Wh e the IRI makes much of the v tues of ma tyrdom as embod ed by the s aughter of Husse n and h s party at the Batt e of Karba a, t recogn zes that v ctory cannot be ach eved so e y by the death of the fa thfu ; as a resu t, the reg me a so emphas zes the hero c warr or qua t es of A , who pa t c pated n near y eve y batt e waged by the Mus m army dur ng h s fet me as a standard-bearer, champ on n one-on-one contests, and bodyguard for the Prophet Muhammad

79 "The Armed M ght of Iran: Ab e to Man fest Itse f n a Threaten ng Manner," *Ettela'at*, September 24, 995, 3, trans ated from Pers an by Gu ve Rosen See a so Steven Ward, "Iran s Cha eng ng V ctory Narrat ve," *Historically Speaking*, Vo 0, No 3, June 2009, 4 -42

80 A foneh,"Sh te Combat Casua t es Show the Dep h of Iran s nvo vement n Syr a"; A foneh, "Max ma Exposure, M n ma Presence: Iran s M ta y Engagement n Iraq"

8 A country w th a recessed deterrent has a the bas c e ements requ red to bu d a bomb (f ss e mater a , a weapons des gn, and the ab ty to produce a dev ce) n a number of weeks or months once a dec s on s taken For the or g ns of the concept of a "recessed deterrent," see: A r Commodore Jasj t S ngh, "Prospects for Nuc ear Pro ferat on," n S Sur (Ed), *Nuclear Deterrence Problems and Perspectives in the1990s* (New York: Un ted Nat ons Inst tute for D sarmament Research, 993) 66

82 In th s way, Iran s nuc ear program may resemb e Ind a s nuc ear program, wh ch served pr mar y po t ca -psycho og ca purposes dur ng ts ear y years George Perkov ch, "What Makes the Ind an Bomb T ck?" n *Nuclear India in the Twenty-first Century*, ed D R Sar Desa and Raju G C Thomas (New York: Pa grave, 2002), 25 60

83 Bennett Ramberg, "Nuc ear Power to the Peop e: The M dd e East s New Go d Rush," *Foreign Affairs*, May 25, 20 5, https://www fore gnaffa rs com/art c es/m dd e-east/20 5-05-25/nuc ear-power-peop e

84 Arash Karam , "Ayato ah Khamene ca s for ar ned st ugg e n West Bank," *Al-Monitor*, Ju y 24, 20 4, http://www a -mon tor com/pu se /or g na s/20 4/07/khamene -ca s-pa est n an-referendum-armed-res stance htm ## xzz3Pu4SUX H

8 N cho as B anford, "Iran, Hezbo ah ga n footho d n Go an He ghts," *The Daily Star*, March 2, 20 5, http://www da ystar com b/News/Lebanon -News/20 5/Mar- 2/290472- ran-hezbo ah-ga n-foo ho d- n-go an ashx

86 Lt Co (Ret) M chae Sega , "Iran Acce erates Arm ng of H zbu ah and Hamas for Poss b e C ash w th Israe ," Jerusa em Center for Pub c Affa rs, December 22, 20 4, http://jcpa org/art c e/ ran-arm ng-h zbu ah-hamas/

87 "Iran an Webs te: Iran an Nuc ear Bomb Spe s Death to Israe ." MEMRI Spec a D spatch No 2820, Feb uary 23, 20 0, http://www memr org /report/en/0/0/0/0/0/807/3989 htm

88 M chae E senstadt, *Glass Houses Iran's Nuclear Vulnerab lities*, The Wash ngton Inst tute for Near East Po cy, Ju y , 20 4, http://www wash ngton nst tute org/up oads/Documents/pubs/G ass_Houses_f na pdf

89 W thout debat ng the concept of "rat ona ty," t s c ear that n matters of war and peace, dec s on makers are often nf uenced by a myr ad of factors that d stort judgment, frequent y w th trag c resu ts Thus, n her c ass c study of fo y the pursu t by eaders or governments of po c es

contrary to the r own nterests the h stor an Barbara W Tuchman states that reason has been "more often than not overpowered by non-rat ona human fra t es amb t on, anx ety, status-seek ng, face-sav ng, us ons, se f-de us ons, f xed prejud ces A though the structure of human thought s based on og ca procedures from prem se to conc us on, t s not proof aga nst the fra t es and the pass ons " Barbara W Tuchman, *The March of Folly From Troy to Vietnam* (New York: A fred A Knopf, 984), 380 For a more recent study by a behav ora econom st who argues that human dec s onmak ng s more often gu ded by emot on than og c, and s rrat ona n systemat c and pred ctab e ways, see: Dan Ar e y, *Predictably Irrational The Hidden Forces that Shape our Decisions* (New York: HarperCo ns, 2008)

[90] Co n H Kah , Raj Pattan , and Jacob Stokes, *If All Else Fails The Challenges of Containing a Nuclear Iran* (Wash ngton DC: Center for a New Amer can Secur ty, 20 3), 20 2 , 50, 52, http://www cnas org/f es/documents/pub cat ons/CNAS_IfA E seFa s pdf

[9] Er k O son, "Iran s Path-Dependent M tary Doctr ne," unpub shed manuscr pt, September 20 5, 26

[92] M chae E senstadt, "Speak ng about the Unth nkab e: The Nuc ear Debate Iran Needs to Have," The Wash ngton Inst tute, *PolicyWatch* 2279, Ju y , 20 4, http://www wash ngton nst tute org/po cy-ana ys s/v ew/speak ng-about-the-unth nkab e-the-nuc ear-debate- ran-needs-to-have

[93] "B ack Swans" are ow-probab ty, h gh- mpact events Nass m N cho as Ta eb, *The Black Swan The Impact of the Highly Improbable* (New York: Random House, 20 0)

[94] Jeffrey Go dberg, "Netanyahu Confronts Obama, and a 'Mess an c Apoca ypt c Cu t ", *The Atlantic*, March 3, 20 5, http://www theat ant c com / nternat ona /arch ve/20 5/03/netanyahu-vs-a-mess an c-apoca ypt c-cu t/386650/

[9] Bernard Lew s, "August 22: Does Iran Have Someth ng n Store?" *Wall Street Journal*, August 8, 2006, http://www wsj com/art c es /SB 5500 54638829470

[96] See, for nstance, Fareed Zakar a, "Deterr ng Iran s the Best Opt on," *Washington Post*, March 4, 20 2, https://www wash ngtonpost com /op n ons/deterr ng- ran- s-the-best-opt on/20 2/03/ 4/gIQA0Y9mCS_sto y htm ; Zb gn ew Brzez nsk nterv ew on A jazeera (Eng sh), "U S and Iran: Best of Enem es," *Empire,* March 3 , 20 0, http://eng sh a jazeera net/programmes/emp re/20 0/03/20 033 3 965 4403 htm For the m tat ons of Co d War mode s of deterrence as app ed to Iran, see Patr ck C awson and M chae E senstadt, eds , *Deterring the Ayatollahs Complications in Applying Cold War Strategy to Iran,* Po cy Focus no 72 (Wash ngton, DC: Wash ngton Inst tute for Near East Po cy, Ju y 2007), http://www wash ngton nst tute org/pubPDFs/Po cyFocus72F na Web pdf

[97] Chub n, "Iran s 'R sk-Tak ng n Perspect ve"

[98] Qa dar , "More p anes, more m ss es, more warsh ps: Iran ncreases ts m tary budget by a th rd"

[99] M chae E senstadt and Brenda Shaffer, "Russ an S-300 M ss es to Iran: Groundhog Day or Game-Changer?" The Wash ngton Inst tute for Near East Po cy, *PolicyWatch* 2482, September 4, 20 5, http://www wash ngton nst tute org/po cy-ana ys s/v ew/russ an-s-300-m ss es-to- ran -groundhog-day-or-game-changer

[200] O son, "Iran s Path-Dependent M tary Doctr ne," 26

[20] Lev tt, *Hizballah and the Qods Force in Iran's Shadow War with the West*

[202] Va Nasr, "Why Conta n Iran When ts Own A ms w Do Just That?" *Bloomberg Views*, October 3 , 20 , http://www b oombergv ew com /a t c es/20 - 0-3 /why-conta n- ran-when- ts-own-a ms-w -do-just-that-va -nasr

[203] E senstadt, Kn ghts, and A , *Iranian Influence in Iraq*

Michael Eisenstadt

[204] Adam Entous and Ju an E Barnes, "U S Bu ks Up Iran Defenses," *Wall Street Journal*, Februa y 25 26, 20 2, A , A8, http://on ne wsj com /a t c e/SB 000 4240529702047786045772436403 7724400 h m

[20] Awad Mustafa, "L tt e Progress Made on Integrated GCC M ss e Sh e d," *Defense News*, August 30, 20 5, http://www defensenews ccm/story /defense/po cy-budget/warfare/20 5/08/30/ tt e-progress-made ntegrated-gcc-m ss e-sh e d/32390269/

[206] E en Nakash ma, "U S Response to Bank Cyberattacks Ref ects D p omat c Caut on, Vexes Bank Indust y," *Washington Post*, Apr 27, 20 3, http://www wash ngtonpost com/wor d/nat ona -secur ty/ s-response-to-bank-cyberattacks-ref ects-d p omat c-caut on-vexes-bank - ndustry/20 3/04/27/4a7 efe2-aea2- e2-98ef-d 072ed3cc27_story htm ; D rector of Nat ona Inte gence James C apper, "Wor dw de Threat Assessment of the U S Inte gence Commun ty" (statemen to the US Senate Se ect Comm ttee on Inte gence, March 2, 20 3), 3, http://www nte gence senate gov/ 303 2/c apper pdf; Nat ona Academy of Sc ences, "Terror sm and the E ectr c Power De very System," November 20 2, http://s tes nat ona academ es org/xped o/grou s/depss te/documents/webpage/deps_073368 pdf

[207] Jeffrey S Lant s, "Strateg c Cu ture and Ta ored Deterrence: Br dg ng the Gap Between Theo y and Pract ce," *Contemporary Security Policy*, Vo 30, No 3 (December 2009), 467-485, http://www contemporarysecur typo cy org/assets/CSP-30-3-Lant s pdf

[208] Jav er B as, "P pe nes bypass ng Hormuz open," *Financial Times*, Ju y 5, 20 2, http://www ft com/cms/s/0/4203f88 -ce83- e -9f 7 -00 44feabdc0 htm #axzz3mLROP3jY

[209] CDR Ryan T Tewe , "Assess ng the U S A rcraft Carr er Gap n the Gu f," The Wash ngton Inst tute for Near East Po cy, *PolicyWatch* 24 7, October 5, 20 5, http://www wash ngton nst tute org/po cy-ana ys s/v ew/assess ng-the-u s-a rcraft-carr er-gap- n-the-gu f; Mark Gunz nger w th Chr s Doughe ty, *Outside-In Operating from Range to Defeat Iran's Anti-Access and Area-Denial Threats* (Wash ngton, D C : Center for Strateg c and Budgetary Assessments, 20), http://www csbao ne org/wp-content/ up oads/20 /0 /CSBA_outs deIn_ebook pdf See a so, M chae E senstadt, "Gett ng Carr er Out of the Gu f Good for U S Iran Po cy," *Defense News*, March 0, 20 3, http://arch ve defensenews com /a t c e/20 303 0/DEFFEAT05/303 00007/Gett ng-Carr er-Out-Gu f-Good-U-S-Iran-Po cy

[2 0] For nstance, n exp a n ng the dep oyment of add t ona forces to the reg on n 20 2, a sen or Defense Depa tment off c a exp a ned that "The message to Iran s, 'Don t even th nk about t Don t even th nk about c os ng the stra t We c ear the m nes Don t even th nk about send ng your fast boats out to harass our vesse s or commerc a sh pp ng We put them on the bottom of the Gu f '" But such an approach perm ts Iran to dec de what k nd of osses t s w ng to ncur n order to ach eve an object ve, and n do ng so, t may effect ve y ower the thresho d for act on Thom Shanker, Er c Schm tt, and Dav d E Sanger, "U S Adds Forces n Pers an Gu f, a S gna to Iran," *New York Times*, Ju y 3, 20 2, http://www nyt mes com/20 2/07/03/wor d/m dd eeast/us-adds-forces- n-pers an-gu f-a-s gna -to- ran htm ?pagewanted a

[2] Po t ca Warfare Execut ve (UK), *The Meaning, Techniques and Methods of Political Warfare*, 942, dec ass f ed manua , f e ref FO 898/ 0 , http://www psywar org/psywar/reproduct ons/MeanTechMethod pdf; George Kennan, "The Inaugurat on of Organ zed Po t ca Wa fare," Apr 30, 948, dec ass f ed memo, http://d g ta arch ve w soncenter org/document/ 4320; Max Boot and M chae Doran, "Department of D rt Tr cks: Why the Un ted States Needs to Sabotage, Underm ne, and Expose Its Enem es n the M dd e East," *ForeignPolicy.com*, June 28, 20 3, http://fore gnpo cy com/20 3/06/28/department-of-d ty-tr cks/

[2 2] Tehran s efforts to restr ct the f ow of nformat on to ts peop e have h ndered, but fa ed to ha t, on ne commun cat ons See, for nstance, Dav d Ho mes, "State of Censorsh p: How Iran Censors the Internet (and How Its C t zens Get around It)," *Pando Daily*, November 2, 20 3 http://pando com/20 3/ / 2/state-of-censorsh p-how- ran-cen ors-the- nternet-and-how- ts-c t zens-get-around- t/ Indeed, some m n ste s see the reg me f ght ng a os ng batt e M chae P zz , "Iran Governm nt M n ster: Med a Bans May Seem 'Laughab e n 5 Years," *Aljazeera America* December 9, 20 3, http://amer ca a jazeera com/art c es/20 3/ 2/ 9/ ran an-m n ster med abansmayseem aughab e n5years htm

[2 3] D on N ssenbaum and Jeffrey Sparshott, "U S Eases Tech Exports to He p Iran an D ssenters," *Wall Street Journal*, May 30, 20 3 http://www wsj com/a t c es/SB 000 424 278873244 26045785 5553 75 76068; Joby Warr ck, "Obama Adm n strat on to He p Iran ans Beat Government Censors," *Washington Post*, May 30, 20 3, http://www wash ngtonpost com/wor d/nat ona -secur ty/obama-adm n strat on-to-he p - ran ans-beat-government-censors/20 3/05/30/94db07b4-c96 - e2-9245-773c0 23c027_story htm

2 4 M chae E senstadt, *The Missing Lever Information Activities Against Iran*, Wash ngton Inst tute for Near East Po cy, Po cy Note No , March 20 0, at: http://www wash ngton nst tute org/pub-PDFs/Po cyNote0 pdf

2 Patr ck C awson, "Iran s Post-Dea Econom c Stagnat on Cha enges Rouhan ," Wash ngton Inst tute for Near East Po cy, *PolicyWatch* 2500, October 8, 20 5, http://www wash ngton nst tute org/po cy-ana ys s/v ew/ rans-post-dea -econom c-stagnat on-cha enges-rouhan

2 6 Bozorgmehr Sharafed n, "Iran s Supreme Leader Bans Negot at ons w th the Un ted States," *Reuters*, October 7, 20 5, http://www reuters com /a t c e/20 5/ 0/07/us- ran-us-ta ks- dUSKCN0S 0P220 5 007

2 7 Dr Ebtesam a -Ketb /Iran an Stud es Un t, *The Doctrinal Foundations of Iran's Geopolitical Project*, Em rates Po cy Center, Po cy Paper No 2, 20 5, 27-3

Michael Eisenstadt

Michael Eisenstadt

About the Author

Michael Eisenstadt is the Kahn Fellow and Director of the Military and Security Studies Program at The Washington Institute for Near East Policy. A specialist in Persian Gulf and Arab-Israeli security affairs, he has published widely on the armed forces of the Middle East and on irregular and conventional warfare and nuclear weapons proliferation in the region.

Prior to joining the Institute in 1989, Mr Eisenstadt worked as a military analyst with the US government. Mr. Eisenstadt served for twenty-six years as an officer in the US Army Reserve before retiring in 2010. His military experience included active-duty service in Iraq, Turkey, Israel, the West Bank, and Jordan, at US Central Command headquarters in Tampa and at the Pentagon.

He has also served in a civilian capacity on the Multinational Force-Iraq/US Embassy Baghdad Joint Campaign Plan Assessment Team (2009) and as a consultant or advisor to the congressionally mandated Iraq Study Group (2006), the Multinational Corps-Iraq Information Operations Task Force (2005-2006), and the State Department's Future of Iraq defense policy working group (2002-2003). In 1992, he took a leave of absence from the Institute to work on the US Air Force Gulf War Air Power Survey.

Mr. Eisenstadt earned an MA in Arab Studies from Georgetown University and has traveled widely in the Middle East.

Acknowledgements

The author would like to thank Dr. Amin Tarzi and Adam Seitz of the Middle East Studies program at Marine Corps University for their support and encouragement, and their deft editorial hand. He would also like to thank Dr. Patrick Clawson, Dr. David Crist, Dr. Mehrdad Haghayeghi, Ambassador John Limbert, and Olivier Decottignies for their extraordinarily insightful and useful comments on earlier drafts of this monograph, and Ian Duff, Benjamin Filreis, Omar Mukhlis, and Guive Rosen for their research assistance.

The Strategic Culture of the Islamic Republic of Iran

Religion, Expediency, and Soft Power in an Era of Disruptive Change

Michael Eisenstadt

In this expanded and revised edition of "The Strategic Culture of the Islamic Republic of Iran," originally published in 2011, Michael Eisenstadt focuses on Iran's unique approach to statecraft, strategy, and the use of force, and distills the core elements of its strategic culture:

- Policy in the theocratic Islamic Republic of Iran (IRI) is, paradoxically, based on the secular concept of raison d'état, rather than on religious or ideological imperatives—though this largely pragmatic approach coexists uneasily with the regime's rigid doctrine of "resistance";

- Iran generally seeks to avoid or deter conventional conflict, while advancing its anti-status quo agenda via proxy and information (i.e., psychological warfare) operations, combining "soft" and "hard" power to advance its national security objectives;

- The IRI has traditionally taken a holistic approach to the employment of "soft" and "hard" power, prioritizing the former over the latter. This may be changing, however, as a result of its recent military interventions in Syria and Iraq;

- To deal with the array of threats it faces, the IRI has created a deterrent and warfighting triad consisting of proxy/unconventional warfare forces, a guerilla navy, and robust rocket and missile forces.

- The IRI's "way of war" emphasizes indirection, ambiguity, and strategic patience; the moral, spiritual, and psychological dimensions of statecraft and strategy; reciprocity, proportionality, and the calibrated use of violence; tactical flexibility; and the creation of wedges in hostile coalitions.

Regarding Tehran's long-term nuclear plans, the study concludes that Iran is likely to eventually continue its pursuit of nuclear weapons, whether or not the recently concluded nuclear deal remains in force.

And while the IRI's leadership has shown that it is "rational" and generally risk averse, it is also occasionally prone to reckless behavior and to overreach—tendencies which its far-reaching ambitions tend to amplify. This could greatly complicate efforts to create a stable deterrent balance with a nuclear Iran.

Middle East Studies
at the Marine Corps University